CLASH OF TWO CULTURES

South Sudanese Refugees Living in Australia

Dhanojak Obongo

Published in the United States of America by SAALAMTA, Inc. Saalamata is a book publishing service working along side promising authors since 1999. For more information contact mae.reggy@beulah.edu

ISBN-13 978 1495913150
ISBN-10 1495913155

Acknowledgements

Special thanks are due to the Rt.Rev. Peter Hollingsworth, of the former Brisbane Anglican Diocese for his generous financial assistance during my post graduate studies.

To Ambassador James Morgan, who also edited some of my articles and provided his esteemed perspective, and to Ambassador Akec Khoc, current South Sudanese Ambassador to the United States for his encouragement during the writing of this book.

To Ms. Melva Queen who was the first person to edit my manuscript on the profile of the Sudanese community in Queensland, Australia back to December 2000 and to Bob Stadellhafer who edited and read my manuscript and provided much appreciated editorial remarks and professional advisement.

To Dr. Mae Reggy of Beulah Heights University who contributed her expertise to the polishing and final editing. Also to Rev. Dr. Robert Norris, of the Fourth Evangelical Presbyterian Church; to Corline Vanduzer in the States; and to Reverend Les Percy in Brisbane who assisted in the editorial process.

To Ms. Neslihan Gunay, my former Secretary in the Sudanese Embassy Ankara, Turkey who first started typing this manuscript; to Miss Nancy Geri who also typed some of the materials I wrote in the USA; to my personal assistant Ms. Nyakan Gile for her help with arranging material. Last but not least to Mr. James Jok Omot who helped me with Nuer spellings and aspects of Nuer culture and to Mr. Luk Dak for encouraging me to write this book.

I also take this opportunity to thank to my wife, Nadia Imam Elias Mogga, my daughter Deborah, and my other children, Joshua and Christina for their assistance and support as I prepared the groundwork for this book. I wish to express my appreciation and thanks to all others who have assisted me in the work. Nevertheless, I take full responsibility for all the opinions expressed in this book.
Dhanojak Obongo, Washington, DC–USA

TABLE OF CONTENTS

Dedication

To the memory of my beloved parents

Foreword

I was born in Akobo District, Jonglei State, South Sudan in 1959. At the time of my birth, many children were dying as vaccinations were not common. Although the naming of children was very important in our culture, my parents did not give me a name because so many children were dying and they were not sure I would survive. So when one of the neighbors asked, "What is this child's name?" My father said, "I don't know. Just call him *dhanojak*" which in the Anyuak language means "an ordinary human." From then on, people called me *dhanojak*. They did not know that events of my life would unfold in ways that are far beyond ordinary.

My mother was a traditional midwife and my father was a blacksmith as well as a butcher in Akobo District. Most of the butchers were Arab-Muslim merchants. Although my father was not an Arab, he was a Muslim. Thus he slaughtered cows using *halal* practices so that the Muslim community could buy the meat. According to Islamic law, the slaughter must be performed by a Muslim, who precedes the slaughter by invoking the name of Allah, most commonly by saying *Bismillah* ("In the name of Allah") and then three times *Allahu akbar* ("God is the greatest"). Then, the cow must be slaughtered with a sharp knife by cutting the throat,

9

windpipe and the blood vessels in the neck (while the cow is alive), causing its death without cutting the spinal cord. Lastly, the blood from the veins must be drained. This is the way that my father earned a living. Whenever he slaughtered cows, he was given a kilo of meat as salary.

I am the only boy amongst my three siblings, namely Rebecca Amot, Opara (now deceased), and Christina Karkon. My beloved parents did not have the advantage of a formal education, but they sent us to school. Like many South Sudanese parents, they believed that education is the only means to overcome poverty and lead a better life. I attended primary school in Akobo District and secondary school in Malakal, a town located on the banks of the White Nile. After graduating from secondary school, I received a scholarship to go to seminary in Cairo, Egypt.

Although I graduated from seminary, I did not become an ordained pastor as expected, but many other doors opened for me. I started working as a secondary school teacher in Khartoum and later as a relief worker. Due to circumstances detailed later in this book, I eventually fled to Addis Ababa where I was designated as an urban refugee and secured the opportunity to resettle in a third country, Australia, as a political refugee.

On the 25th of November, 1997, I arrived in Brisbane, Australia with Hellen, my wife at that time, and our four children Leacha, Obongo, Simon and Anderson. Brisbane is the capital and most populous city in the Australian State of Queensland and the third most populous city the entire country. We were among the first group of refugees from Sudan/South Sudan to arrive there. As part of my volunteer experience, I worked at the Multicultural Development Association (MDA), an agency working with refugees in general, and Sudanese/South Sudanese refugees in the particular. There was a story to tell.

The majority of Sudanese/South Sudanese refugees who migrated to Australia and other parts of the globe fled their home country due to political and religious persecution as well as the violation of human rights. Due to the military junta and militant Islamic fundamentalist regime with its poor human rights records, many south/South Sudanese were given the opportunity by both the United Nations High Commission for Refugee (UNCHR) and the Australian Federal Government to resettle in Australia. A great number were forced to live in squalid refugee camps in neighboring countries before resettling in Australia.

When they arrived in Australia, many of the settlers from Sudan/South Sudan knew little or no English and needed assistance finding employment. Some families were large and had trouble finding suitable accommodations. In addition to that, a greater sense of freedom in Australia changed traditional authority relationships and caused conflict within Sudanese/South Sudanese families and communities. Australian welfare systems also caused conflicts in some families, especially providing youth allowances at age 18. Western-style dress also challenged traditional values and norms. In short, the newly arrived Sudanese/South Sudanese refugees faced many resettlement challenges and the Australian community also faced challenges providing services to these newcomers to their country

From the beginning, my purpose was to write a research paper that would provide the Multicultural Development Association (MDA) with background information—social and political—about South Sudanese refugees who were then the majority are living in Brisbane, Queensland State. The idea was to both advocate and educate on behalf of the South Sudanese Community about the social, political and historical background of the Civil War in Sudan.

Currently the Sudanese/South Sudanese community is one of the fastest growing immigrant groups in

Australia. According to the 2011 Australian census, there are currently 30,000 Sudanese/South Sudanese living in Australia. According to community leaders, 31,000 Sudanese/South Sudanese currently live in Canada and 90,000 to 100,000 Sudanese/South Sudanese currently live in the United States. It is my hope in writing this book is that it will be of significance to refugee service providers working with the Sudanese/South Sudanese community in Australia, and more broadly, that it will be a resource for all NGOs and government officials working with refugees and immigrants, especially Sudanese/South Sudanese immigrants in other parts of the world.

In the book, I also have a chapter to address the conflict between my two beloved communities; namely, the indigenous Ciro-Anyuak of Akobo, and the Lou-Nuer-Mor (now settled in Akobo for almost five decades). I have provided this humble perspective with the hope that it will be a significant contribution in the effort to resolve the conflict between these two communities.

Chapter 1

Historical Background of the Two Sudans

Sudan was the largest country in the African continent before split of the Republic of South Sudan (RSS). In the Arabic language, the name *Sudan* means "land of the black." A historian once said, "This terminology was first applied by Arab geographers, to define the localities involving the south of the Sahara in Africa."

Sudan can be divided into three geographical regions. The northern part of Sudan is a desert and semi-desert area. The central part of Sudan supports much of the country's agriculture and consists of vast plains broken up by occasional hills. The southern part of Sudan is thick tropical rain forest (Barsella, C.1998). Among the marvelous geographical features of Sudan are the White and Blue Nile Rivers and their tributaries. Former Sudan was surrounded by nine countries, namely Libya and Egypt in the North; Chad, Central Africa and Congo (formerly Zaire) in the West; Uganda, Kenya, Ethiopia and Eritrea in the East.

Between 1885 and 1956, Sudan was ruled by British administration, while Egypt was a junior partner in the administration. On 1st January 1956 Sudan received its independence from Great Britain. Sudan is a member of the former Organization of African Unity (OAU) currently known as the Africa Union (AU)), and the Arab League as well as a member of the United Nations Organization (UNO).

The First Rebellion of Torit 1955

Sudan's political history has been unstable. The first civil war was started on 18th August 1955 by a group of Southern Sudanese soldiers. It was the starting point of the civil conflict in Sudan. The conflict in South Sudan was more a political one than a religious conflict (Barsella, 1998).

The Second Civil War

In May 1983, again a group of Southern Sudanese soldiers rebelled against the Government of Sudan (GOS), because of the absence of development in Southern Sudan and violation of the Addis Abba Accord (AAA). This Accord gave Southern Sudan Regional Self-government within united Sudan. Also the imposition of the Islamic Law (*Sharia*) was the other cause of the second civil war in Sudan (Alier, 1991).

The great numbers of Sudanese/South Sudanese refugees in Australia, and particularly in Queensland are the product of the political crisis in Sudan from 1983 to 2005. On the whole, they are political refugees due to political and religious persecution, as well as the violation of human rights in Sudan (Amnesty International Report 1995). During the second civil war, approximately two million people died and there were four to five million internally displaced persons, probably the largest figure in the globe at that time (Sudan Democratic Gazette, April 2000).

The Current Regime in Sudan

The current regime in Sudan came to power on 30 June 1989. They took the power from the democratically elected civilian government. The present regime is led by the military-Islamic fundamentalist junta under General-Omar Hassen Al-Bashir. This regime is described by the international community as the most extremist Islamic regime on the African continent and the whole Middle east area. Sudan is among those countries labelled by the US State Department, as a terrorist country or one which encourages and sponsors international terrorism in the world today. Moreover, in 1997 during President Bill Clinton's administration, the United States imposed the embargo over Sudan's alleged support for international terrorism and human rights violations.

Two Marginalized States in Northern Sudan

The Southern Kordfan State is also known as the Nubia Mountains, while the Blue Nile State known as Fung. People from these two areas joined the Sudan People's Liberation Army/Movement (SPLA/M) in 1980s because they felt that their areas were marginalized by the Arabized Muslim Central Government since independence of Sudan in 1956. Sudanese people from the Nubian Mountains and people of Fung (Blue Nile) are very proud to be Africans despite the fact that the majority of them are Muslims.

The resolution of the above mentioned states by the two partners named the SPLM and NCP was based on economic, political, social and administration answers to the question of the Blue Nile and the Nuba Mountains. Thus, the resolution of the two states has given them a chance to reflect on their heterogeneous traditions and to develop their native languages and moreover, to develop their resources as a way to encourage sustainable development in these two northern states.

The most important gain that these two states achieved from the Comprehensive Peace Agreement (CPA) in 2005 was that in four years from the signing of the CPA, the two states would elect their legislative assemblies democratically. The resolution stipulated that, each state legislative assembly (Parliament) shall form an Assembly Assessment and Evolution Commission (AAEC) to evaluate and judge the fulfillment of the accord in each state. Furthermore, the CPA indicated that an independent commission shall be formed by the Presidency to evaluate and judge the accomplishment of the CPA in the two states. This Commission will give its accounts to the Federal Government and the governments of the two States.

The first term of the (CPA) rotation of 18 months in 2005s was given to the SPLM in Southern Kordofan while the Blue Nile State Governorship was taken by the NCP. However, when the election was conducted in April 2010, the SPLM under the leadership of commander, Mr. Malek Agar won the Governorship for the duration of five years in the Blue Nile State. It is worth mentioning here that the National Census was not conducted in the Southern Kordofan State, due to the dispute between the two peace-partners the SPLM and the NCP over distribution of seats. In 2010 the National Census was carried out and its results were recognized by the Presidency or in other words by the two peace-partners SPLM and the NCP. In 2011, it was expected that partial elections will be conducted specifically to elect the Governor and the State Assembly Members of Parliament (MPs) respectively. According to the CPA, in the Southern Kordofan as well as the Blue Nile State, the power sharing was distributed as follows:

1- Fifty-five percent (55%)to the NCP.

2- Forty-five percent (45%) to the SPLM.

While the CPA stipulated that, the Blue Nile and the Southern Kordofan shall be equally represented in the Federal Institution according to population. Commander Mr. Khamis Ismail Jalab was the first son of the Nuba Mountains to become the Governor after the signing of the CPA.

The Sudan Referendum: One Country or Two?

On Sunday 9th January, 2011 the South Sudanese inside Sudan and in the Diaspora went to the polls in the early morning to cast their ballots in the first ever historical referendum to decide between united Sudan and secession. The first person to cast his vote was His Excellency Mr. Salva Kiir Mayardit, first Vice President of Sudan and President of the Government of Southern Sudan (GOSS) by then, and currently, the first President of a newly born nation since its Declaration of Independence on 9th July 2011.

Several voters queued up in the middle of the night, and some slept at the site of late hero of Dr. John Garang's cemetery where President Salva Kiir voted. In his message, Mr. Kiir told the crowd of Southern Sudanese people, "I am sure that those who died didn't die in vain." He went on to tell them, "This is the historic moment the people of Southern Sudan have been waiting for."

The referendum voting continued from the 9th January to 16th January 2011. Tens of thousands of Southern

Sudanese in the Diaspora voted including those in Australia which had nine thousand registered voters. The referendum voting was conducted in USA, Canada and Australia and some African countries.

After counting the votes, the results showed that the South Sudanese had voted overwhelmingly for the secession. It was recognized first by the GOS and the whole world followed suit. Thus, the Republic of South Sudan became the 192nd member of the United Nations Organization (UNO) and 54th member of the African Union (AU).

Chapter 2

General Background of the Two Sudans

Size and Population

The size of Sudan before the independence of the Republic of South Sudan was one million square miles. The former Sudan was equivalent to the size of the Western Australia. According to 2010 Sudan census, the population of Sudan was estimated to be about 40 million inhabitants. The yearly estimated population growth between 1990 and 1998 was 2.0 per cent (UNAIDS/WHO2000 Update). This puts present estimates of the population of Sudan after the secession of South Sudan at a little over 30 million people.

The Republic of Sudan is composed of people from diverse religious, cultural, and linguistic backgrounds (Deng, Francis 1994). Sudanese Africans are by far the largest ethnic group in Sudan. They are almost entirely Muslims while Arabs are the minority group. Sudan also hosts a large refugee population. The majority of the refugee population came from Eritrea, Chad, Ethiopia, and the Central African Republic.

The Republic of South Sudan is about a quarter of a million square miles in area. This is slightly smaller than the state of Texas, USA. The Republic of South Sudan has an estimated population of nearly 8.5 million. The population is a mixture of languages and ethnicities e.g. Nilotic,

http://unmiss.unmissions.org/LinkClick.aspx?fileticket=-cHImu5Aea0%3d&tabid=5083&language=en-USNilo-Hamitic and the South-Western Sudanic groups.

- **Nilotic group**: Includes the Dinka (largest, with estimated population of over 1 million), Acholi, Anyuak, Bor-Belanda (Jor), Dembo, Shatt, Shilluk (Collo), Pari, and Nuer.

- **Nilo-Hamitic group**: Includes the Bari, Beir, Buya, Didinga, Domjing, Jiye, Kakwa, Kuku, Lango, Latuko, Logit, Lokoya, Lopit, Luluba, Mundari, Murle, Nyangwara, Nyepo, Pojulu, Tennet, Toposa, Lokoya and Makaraka , etc.

- **The Sudanic group:** Includes Avukaya, Azande, Biri, Baka, Balanda,, Bongo, Feroge, Kresh, Madi, Makaraka, Moru, Muru, Mundo, Ndogo, and Sere,

The major religions are Christianity and African traditional religions plus a sizable number of adherents of the Muslim community.

Capital Cities

Khartoum is the capital and largest city of the Republic of Sudan. It is located at the place where the White Nile flowing north from Lake Victoria and the Blue Nile flowing west from Ethiopia come together. Divided by the White and Blue Niles, Khartoum is growing rapidly and has an estimated population of over five million people. In the Arabic language, the name *Khartoum* means "elephant tusks."

Juba is the capital and largest city of the Republic of South Sudan. The city is situated on the White Nile and has been developing since the inception of the new nation. As of 2011, the population of the city of Juba was estimated at approximately 372,410.

Economy and Politics

The backbone of the South Sudanese economy is agriculture. South Sudan has arable agricultural land that can make the region a potential breadbasket for the whole of East Africa. Subsistence agriculture provides a living for the majority of the population. The key cash crop is cotton. The government of South Sudan derives nearly 98% of its budget revenues from oil. Besides oil, South Sudan also enjoys other natural resources including fisheries, forestry, animals, and wild life.

Oil is exported through two pipelines that run to refineries and shipping facilities at Port Sudan on the Red Sea. The 2005 oil sharing agreement with Khartoum called for sharing of oil revenues between the two countries. That deal expired on 9th July 2011 when South Sudan became an independent country. Following independence, South Sudan exited with 75% of the oil revenue. However, the economy of South Sudan remains linked to Sudan due to the lack of infrastructure and great expense required to build another pipeline. The Sudanese/South Sudanese economies are in bad shape and suffering simply because of the closed down oil pipe lines terminating export of oil from landlocked South Sudan.

South Sudan economic indicators are as follows:

Economic Indicators	South Sudan	Sub-Saharan Africa(Average)
GDP (millions US $)	12,296	29,000
Inflation (average, %)	45	8
Social Categories:		
Poverty incidence (% of Households)	51	48
Infant mortality rate (% of 1,000 live births	102	68
Prevalence of under nourishment (% of population)	47	25
Literacy rate (% of adult population)	27	68
Access to an improved source (% of population)	55	70

SOURCE: National Bureau of Statistics , South Sudan and IMF staff estimates.

Facing problems of poverty and lack of infrastructure, South Sudan needs to consider diversifying its economy to minimize threats from its northern neighbor. In the future, the problem of money in South Sudan will not be an issue, but the long-term consideration will be financial management of revenue, focusing on macroeconomic stability and improving the business environment as well as eradicating corruption from politicians and civil servants.

Education

The Sudanese/South Sudanese like other people in the world take education very seriously, as a means to combat poverty. In the early 1920's up to the 1960's the English language was the language of instruction in all levels of education including primary and secondary schools. However, when Sudan gained its independence in 1956, the Arabization and Islamization policies were imposed by the GOS of the day.

Arabization and Islamization describe the cultural influence that imposed the Arabic language, and Islamic culture on non-Arab, non-Muslim local populations. As a result of Arabization and Islamization policies, Arabic became the language of instruction at the primary and secondary levels. English only remained as the language of instruction at the higher education level in Sudan. In 1990's

27

the current Islamic Military junta Arabitized and Islamized all institutions of higher education, making Arabic the language of instruction for the whole system of education throughout the country.

In 1969, when former President Nimiery came to power, he introduced what the regime called the "educational ladder" (i.e. six years primary, three years, junior secondary and three years senior secondary school.) When the current regime seized the power in Sudan in 1989, they transformed the educational ladder from the above 6+3+3 to two year at pre-school, eight years at basic level and three years at senior secondary school (2+8+3) in the 1990s. As mentioned earlier, the current Islamic Military junta under President of Sudan introduced Arabization and Islamization policies. Subsequently, the Arabic language was adopted as the official language of instruction from the primary level through the university level throughout Sudan and the entire curriculum was written in the Arabic language as well.

Adult Literacy

UNESCO estimated that the total adult population (ages 15 and above) who can read and write in Sudan was 71.9 % in 2009. The literacy rate for adult males was 80.7% and 63.2% for adult females. This was before the succession of South Sudan (2011). It is also estimated that total adult population (ages 15 and above) who can read and write in South Sudan is 27 %. The literacy rate for adult males was 40% and 16% for adult females.

Female Education

Education in Sudan, in general, has been male-dominated. In North Sudan, which is predominantly Muslim and Arab culture, education is frequently offered in a religious school known as a *khalwa* where the Holy Koran/ *Quran* is taught to children. In most cases, girls have not been enrolled in these *khalwa*. With the initiative and advocacy of Sheik Bakrey Badri, in 1920 the Colonial Government of Sudan (GOS) established five elementary schools for girls. In 1940, the colonial regime of the day established the first intermediate school for girls. On the eve of Sudanese Independence in 1956, the first secondary school for girls was opened in Omdurman, the secondary school being for the whole of Sudan. Sheik Bakrey Badri also opened the Ahfad University College in Omdurman for girls in the 1920s.The Ahfad University College was the only female higher education institute and university in the land by then and today.

Despite the improvement in girl's education in the Muslim and Arabic areas of Sudan, it was not the same in

South Sudan. Among Africans, both Christian and adherents of African traditional religion, the precedent of girl's education continued roughly as it was. When ex-president Nimery took power in 1969, there were some slight improvements in girls' educational standards, and particularly girl's education in South Sudan.

The reason behind the state of female education in Sudan/South Sudan goes back to the conception among parents that education will result in untrustworthy behavior in girls. In other words, parents tended to believe that education causes girls to become resistant to following conservative traditions. From this argument, the males managed to obtain the lion's share of education in the two Sudans.

Female Rights

Abuse of female rights was common in Northern Sudan, particularly in the Sudanese capital of Khartoum. Females confronted genuine bans on their liberty. For example, the Public Order Act of Khartoum 1992 as well as the imposition of Islamic Law (*Sharia*) does not allow female merchants to appear in public localities before 5 a.m. or after 5 p.m. No such ban applies to males. A visa for a female to go outside of Sudan was granted only when written permission was given by a male guardian. Command over a female's body, their children as well as their property was the responsibility of their male guardian. Abuse against the female within the household took place with virtual impunity (Amnesty International Report on Sudan, 1999).

In September 2000, the Government of Sudan issued a Republic degree, prohibiting females from public work localities (Sudan Democratic Gazette, October 2000). Females are the most jeopardized among the jeopardized communities in Sudan. All of these bans, laws and rules are applied to all Sudanese females. Whether they are Christians or Muslims, they are all treated alike.

Laws

Before Arabization and Islamization policies of the Sudan, most of the laws were adopted from the English laws. Since May 1983, the Government of Sudan (GOS) brought in a change. Sudanese laws became more Islamic in accordance with the Islamic Laws (*Sharia*), including cutting of a hand as a penalty for theft as well as hanging. Capital punishment is still practiced in the Sudan.

Health

South Sudanese have very poor access to health care. There is a shortage of hospitals and skilled health workers and a limited supply of medicines and equipment. According to the Ministry of Health, South Sudan has about

120 medical doctors and just over 100 registered nurses for an estimated population of early nine million people. Vulnerable groups like women, children and the elderly are particularly at risk. South Sudan has the highest maternal mortality rate in the world. (ICRC, 2012)

As South Sudan is a part of the developing world, malnutrition and epidemics are very common, especially during the 22 years of civil war. Outbreaks of meningitis, measles, yellow fever, and whooping cough are prevalent in many areas. Preventable diseases such as malaria and acute respiratory infections are rampant. River blindness, sleeping sickness, and cholera are also common.

In 1996 research carried out by the Ministry of Health in conjunction with the World Health Organization (WHO) found that five per cent of females tested were HIV positive in Khartoum, capital of Sudan (UNAIDS/WHO, 2000 update). On 27th June 2013, WHO said recent statistics indicate that the number of people in Sudan living with HIV/AIDS has gone up. (www.sudantribune.com/spip.php?article 47140). While in the RSS, I believe the people living with HIV/AIDS will be higher indeed.

Another issue is the estimated 50,000 people in South Sudan with physical disabilities, which are often due to injuries sustained in connection with the armed conflict.

Landmines, already common in the pre-independence armed conflict between the north and the south, are still there today.

Recreation

The Sudanese generally can be described as good and lively conversationalists. Beside conversation and discussion activities, the most fundamental recreation is dancing. In urban areas, dancing and music are the key recreational and social activities. The Sudanese people also love to play football or soccer.

Chapter 3

Ethnicities in the Two Sudans

What makes a huge difference between the Muslim/ Arab Sudanese North and the African Christian-Animist South is the social conditioning of the people. Sudan is unified by salient cultural features—namely the Islamic religion, Arabic language, and above all, Arabic culture. Politically, the population looks to the Arab League for political motivation and encouragement. However the South Sudanese people are oriented towards African tribal/clan ethnic cultures. They have nothing in common with the north except injustice, marginalization and prejudice against them by every Arab/Muslim Regime which has been in power in Khartoum since the so-called Independence of Sudan in 1956. Sudan was a state founded on artificial boundaries from Great Britain which was the historical colonial master power in the Sudan. As in the case of many other African countries, these boundaries were imposed by the colonial powers and not rooted in the will of the people.

Languages

Language Group of Dinka (Monjung) is:

1. Rek-Dinka: include Malual Giernyang_of Awiel, Gogrial and Tonj clans. In Australia, most of the Rek-Dinka are found, in Toowoomba, Adelaide, and Brisbane.

2. Agaar-Dinka (Rumbek) – most of them live in Sydney, Brisbane and .Perth

3. Greater-Bor-Dinka, known sometimes as Jongeli Dinka, are the most political influential and well educated group among other Dinka clans. The majority of them live in South Australia, Tasmania, Queensland, Victoria, and New South Wales, but the biggest center is in Toowoomba, Queensland.

Bari speaking groups are:

Composed of seven ethnicities, namely:

1. Pojulu - found in Brisbane and Melbourne.
2. Kuku - found in Adelaide
3. Kakwa
4. Bari - in Brisbane and Perth
5. Mundari
6. Nyangwara
7. Lolubo

Nuer

Its major clans are:

1. Lou-Nuer predominately in Brisbane. (Mor and Gong Clans)
2. Gajaak-Nuer predominately in Melbourne.

3. Gajook-Nuer predominately in Melbourne and Brisbane (They are the most educated among the Nuer ethnic group.)

4. Laak-Nuer

5. Gawar-Nuer

Padang-Dinka Linguistic Clans are:

1. Abeyi Nyok predominately in Brisbane, Adelaide and Sydney.

2. Panaru

3. Alor

4. Abialang

5. Nyiel

6. Dongiol

7. Luac

8. Thoi

Bor Dinka Clan Group:

Is composed of,

1. Bor - Athuai and Gok they are found in Adelaide, Brisbane and Toowoomba.

2. Nyarweng

3. Hol - found in Brisbane

4. Twic East- found in Sydney, Melbourne, Brisbane and Adelaide

Luo:

Are composed of,

1. Shilluk (Collo) -Nyikango.

2. Luo-Dimuo - known as Jurchol
3. Anyuak (Anywaa) - Gilo.
4. Acholi
5. Pari

The only three tribal kingdoms still existing in South Sudan are the Shilluk, the Anyuak and the Azende (pronounced Zande) one of the largest ethnic groups.

Most ethnicities of South Sudan esteem themselves highly. They are known to be proud, not easily demeaned; especially the Nilotes, who are prepared to protect themselves from any injustice. They are self-reliant, good warriors and sometimes aggressive. Because of this, it is evident that South Sudanese have opposed any kind of colonialism, assimilation and absorption.

Religion

The religious practices among the Sudanese before the arrival of Islam and Christianity were based on the ancient African traditional religions. These African traditional religions were basically animistic. Everything in life—good or bad—was somehow attributed to the actions of gods, spirits or ancestors. This has had a tremendous influence on the practices of Islam and Christianity. For instance, it can be seen that some African Sudanese Muslims still go to practices of African traditional belief such as *alfkey* (sorcery), which has no place in the Holy Koran/*Quran* or in the *Hadith*, prophetic tradition (*Ihadith*).

The different Christian denominations, namely Roman Catholic, American Mission which later become known as the Presbyterian Church (PC/USA), the Church Missionary Society (CMS), under the Anglican Church (United Kingdom), have evangelized the black Sudanese Africans for more than five decades. Ethnic groups in South Sudanese have readily embraced Christianity. This is probably because, embedded in these tribal cultures, there are some practices and understandings which can be found in the Christian faith. For example, many South Sudanese tribal people were born in a barn. The Anyuak are cattle owners and the barn (*lwaga*) is the place where their cattle are kept warm. Anyuak women often gave birth there to keep their babies warm. So the concept of the birth of Jesus Christ in a stable is not a foreign concept at all. The angels announcing Jesus' birth to shepherds does not seem strange to them. As one man said, "When I heard that God sent angels first to the shepherds to announce the birth of His Son Jesus, then I knew He really loves people like us." The traditional use of blood and water is also close to the Christian belief. In the African traditional religion, blood and water are used for sacrifices to protect people against evil spirits. When people want reconciliation between ethnic groups, blood and water are also used. So many ethnicities can easily understand the Christian teaching "Without the shedding of blood, there is no remission of sins." Because blood is essential in the traditional religion, the Christian concept of redemption through the blood of Jesus can be easily embraced by South Sudanese.

As a result of missionary influence, Sudanese/South Sudanese church leaders estimate that 80 percent of the people in the South Sudan are Christians, while there are approximately one million Christians alone in the Nubia Mountains. These are members of Christian denominations mainly the Sudanese Church of Christ (SCOC) which is Baptist-oriented, and the largest church in the Nubia Mountains.

Although South Sudanese communities have embraced Christianity, religious syncretism prevails. That is, the practice of Christianity is mixed with elements of African traditional religion. South Sudanese Christians believe in One Supreme God who created heaven and earth, and lives in heaven. He has different names according to the different ethnic communities and tribal languages. In Anyuak, he is called *Jwok*. In Nuer, he is called *Kouth*. In Dinka, he is called *Naithic*. In all of these communities, Christians acknowledge

Almighty God as sacred and holy, but they still believe in lesser gods who exist in those to whom power is delegated through witchcraft. Whenever bad things occur, the cause is related to the dominion of evil spirits. Thus, in times of crises many practicing South Sudanese Christians still turn to traditional African beliefs such as witchcraft instead of reading their Bible, praying and adhering to Christian doctrines.

It should be noted that some churches openly embrace religious syncretism as a legitimate expression of "Africanized" or "Contextualized" Christianity whereas other churches respond to the charge of religious syncretism more defensively, as they believe that it undermines basic claims of Christianity.

Impact of the Missionaries

The impact of globalization on the South Sudan did not commence in the 21st century. Western missionaries come to Africa with differing specialized knowledge and skills. They included veterinarians, medical doctors, nurses, teachers, translators, agriculturalists and so on. All of these areas of specialization had strong influence on the life styles of South Sudanese people. Missionaries introduced Western modern medicine. Several customs were learned from Western missionaries. In those days, traditional people wore animal skins. The custom of wearing clothes was adopted from Western missionaries who taught people to dress well and keep clean.

Western missionaries greatly impacted education among the ethnicities in South Sudan. Before Sudanese Independence from the Condominium Administration of Great Britain and Egypt, most of the schools in South Sudan were run by missionaries who encouraged the tribal chiefs and nobles to send their children to school. This schooling benefited their children and following the example of tribal chiefs and nobles, the rest of the parents followed suit and sent their children to school. The missionaries also introduced the "Bush Schools" where pupils were taught using the vernacular languages as the medium of instruction for three years. After passing tests, pupils were transferred to the regular school system.

Prior to Independence, the missionaries designed their own curriculum far from the Ministry of Education. When the Sudan obtained its Independence in 1956, the two systems operated side by side, namely the Southern Sudan Curriculum in which the medium of instruction was English, and the so-called National Curriculum in the north which used Arabic as the medium of instruction.

The policies of Arabization and Islamization were introduced to make Sudan, the country of multiculturalism, become a monolithic State. This is the reason why there have been wars of visions in Sudan, since 18th August 1955, right up to January 2005. The people of the Sudan, as a people living in hope expected that the Comprehensive Peace Agreement (CPA) which was signed in Nairobi, Kenya in 2005 would re-write, restructure and re-shape Sudan to accommodate all races and ethnicities in a culturally diverse, and democratic new Sudan. Otherwise, the unity of Sudan would be jeopardized, and that is exactly what happened as the results of the referendum in 2010.

One of the greatest achievements of the Western missionaries was helping local communities put their languages in a written form. For generations, tribal languages were spoken, but not written. Help from indigenous language speakers enabled Western missionaries to introduce orthographies—standardized systems for writing each particular language. As a result, the languages of the indigenous people have been preserved as well as their culture, rich heritage and above all their identity.

With the development of orthographies, Bible translation projects were undertaken. Local South Sudanese people were trained to do the actual translation work. As a result, the Holy Bible was translated into most South Sudanese languages. The availability of the Holy Bible in South Sudanese languages served as a motivation for adult literacy and gave rise to other printed materials such as local language dictionaries. The missionaries' roles were to provide knowledge of the biblical/theological and pedagogical contexts and provide financial support for Bible translation and adult literacy projects.

Slavery

It may take readers of this book by surprise to hear about the practice of slavery in the 21st century in a country like the Sudan. Yet, it is not a myth but it is a reality. During 20 years of civil war, the Arab militias of Darfur and Kordofan in western Sudan captured into slavery Dinka women and children of Northern Bahr Al-Ghazal in Southern Sudan. Since April 2000 the Christian Solidarity International (CSI), a Swiss NGO, has redeemed 5,000 Dinka females and children who had been enslaved by the Northern Sudanese Arabs militias. According to the Sudan Democratic Gazette magazine published monthly in London, UK, by the former Minister of Information and Culture, Mr. Bona Malwal, the redemptions were observed by many groups of Western reporters from Germany and Holland (Sudan Democratic Gazette April, 2000.)

Who are the Lost Boys and Girls?

The origin of the lost boys and girls saga came in May 1983 when civil war erupted between Sudan and South Sudan. Many children were separated from their parents who had been killed by the Arab Islamic regime in Khartoum or war- related effects of hunger, starvation, and disease.

The majority of these boys and girls came from the greater Bahar-El Ghazal region and the Western part of the greater Upper Nile region and were of the Nuer ethnic group.

Some of them managed to flee on foot from the hell of civil war to neighboring countries like Ethiopia and Kenya to refugee camps seeking peace and security. Many died of hunger, dehydration, and illness incurred in long treks toward safety. Most of them were unaccompanied male minors and many of them were unfortunately conscripted by South Sudan's Liberation Army as army fighters against the Arab Islamic government in Khartoum.

In 1999 the concept of resettlement arose with openings from countries like Australia, Canada, and the United States of America. The common criteria were that the children must be orphans. The majority of these estimated 20,000 lost boys and girls of South Sudan were from the Nuer and Dinka ethnic communities.

In 2005 a peace agreement was concluded with the Islamic regime and on July 9, 2011 South Sudan became an independent nation. A sizeable number of South Sudanese refugees in the Diaspora and many lost boys and girls returned to participate in development and reconstruction of their beloved new nation. Some who received the golden opportunity to resettle in the Western world have done well but unfortunately some have gone astray.

Their stories are not over and have been well documented in the United States by two CBS Television documentaries of the Sixty Minutes program narrated by Bob Simon.

Chapter 4

Settling in Australia

How I Became a Refugee

Prior becoming a refugee in Ethiopia and Kenya and before going to resettlement in Australia, I began working with the national Ministry of Education in Khartoum, Sudan, as a secondary school teacher, teaching Christian religious education. At the same time from 1988 to 1992,   I also worked as an administrator with the British Christian relief organization, Christian Outreach, based in Khartoum, Sudan.

In 1992, I received a job opportunity with the United Nations World Food Program, Operation Lifeline Sudan (UN/WFP/OLS) to serve in the northern sector as a relief worker and food monitor in Pochalla County, Jonglei State, South Sudan, after Pochalla town was recaptured from the South Sudanese rebel SPLA.

The day after I arrived in Pochalla in February 1992, a C130 airplane from Lokichoggio, Northern Kenya landed with 500 sacks of sorghum and cooking oil. I met with NGOs to explain the policy of distribution of UN/WFP and the nature of cooperation expected between them and UN/WFP representatives.   Unfortunately, when they distributed the relief items, desired policy was ignored. I raised this matter in our weekly relief meeting several times, but it fell on deaf ears.   Obviously most of these NGOs were loyalists and informants of the Islamic regime in Khartoum.

As an UN/WFP relief administrator and food monitor, I worked in collaboration with the Sudanese indigenous non-governmental organizations (NGOs). Al-Dawa Alslamyia, an Islamic African Relief Agency (IARA) and the Sudanese Red Crescent served as the overall head of the Sudanese NGOs in the area   The UN/WFP was in charge of delivering food and relief supplies to Pochalla County, but the Sudanese indigenous organizations were in charge of distribution. The United Nation's philosophy and policy was that those in charge of distributing food and relief supplies should not discriminate on the basis of race, religion, or gender. However, the above mentioned Islamic NGOs ignored United Nations policy and principles in actual distribution and based their actions on the principle of Islamic conversion, contrary to the rules. For instance, prior to my arrival at Pochalla town, the Islamic Sudanese NGOs were distributing food and relief supplies. They asked anyone who wanted to receive relief items to attend Muslim prayers five times each day. After each prayer, each person received a tin can of sorghum or *dura* as a reward for participating in Islamic religious rites.

Because of political persecution and an attempt on my life by the GOS Islamist agents, on 25th July 1994 I escaped by night from Pochalla crossing Ethiopian border to Gambella, Ethiopia with three companions. After two days walking, we arrived in Pinyudo, Ethiopia, and the following day we proceeded to Gambella, which was the regional 12 headquarters, and an area predominately ruled by Anyuak ethnic elite. This is the area where the author's ancestors come from.

After I escaped, the UN/WFP/OLS in Khartoum realized that they were not receiving any messages from me for a few days. So they informed all their offices: "Dhanojak has disappeared from Pochalla." Soon after, they received this response from their office in Addis Ababa: "Dhanojak is in prison in Gambella." I was accused of being an SPLA officer. Despite presentation of my UN/WFP identity card to the Ethiopian security authorities, they imprisoned me for six months without charges along with my three colleagues: Mr. Moses Ajak, the senior local administrator; Mr. Ojo Okony Okango, a police sergeant; both officials working in Pochalla, County, and the late Thomas Owar Daniel, a student.

After six months we were released without any charges. We went to the United Nations High Commission for Refugees (UNCHR) Gambella branch seeking political asylum from the Ethiopian Government. Asylum was awarded and we were transported to and settled in the Pinyudo refugee camp. However, I decided to go to Addis Ababa with the hope that I would be reinstated to my job by the UN/WFP. But that did not happen. I was given refugee status in Addis Ababa, being designated as an urban refugee

In 1995, I was recommended by Rt. Reverend Matthew Mathiang Deang of the Presbyterian Church of Sudan (PCOS), to work with the New Sudan Council of Churches (NSCC). From 1995-1997, I served as a Relief Co-coordinator for the Upper Nile Region. In 1997, I secured an opportunity for resettlement in a third country, Australia, as a political refugee and moved to Brisbane with my family late that year. [1]

Arriving in Australia

On the 25th of November, 1997, I arrived in Brisbane, Australia with my wife, and our five children, Leacha (age 15), Obongo (age 13), Simon (age 10), Master Anderson (18 months old) and my step-brother Owar (age 17). At the airport, we entered into a sea of white faces—all seemed to be smiling at us as we gathered our luggage from the carousel. Coming from a tropical climate, we had been

---

1

warned that Western countries could be excessively cold during the winter months of November, December, January and February. So we prepared for the cold weather. We were surprised to find that Brisbane was hot!

We were warmly received at the Brisbane International Airport by our support group. From the airport, we were taken to the Aspley Motel for three days, while our support group prepared for our long term accommodation in the suburb of Fitzgibbon, north metropolitan Brisbane. Upon completion of an interview with Centre Link (Social Welfare) at their Chermside office, we were taken to see our new home.

The Fitzgibbon suburb was new and the homes on the estate had just been completed. We were allotted a four bedroom house. The rooms were still brand new, as we were the first tenants to occupy the house. All of us were impressed with such clean and spacious accommodations. Our house in Nairobi, Kenya consisted of two small bedrooms with double deck beds.

My children and I had a good command of the English language. So we did not have a lot of challenges. Only my wife had to learn English. Knowing English made our settlement transitional period very much easier. However, for a few days we struggled with some unfamiliar things such as how to obtain tickets from the ticket machine at the railway station.

It is worth mentioning here that the North Point Refugee Support Group from the Anglican Church under the leadership of the Reverend John Davies was very helpful indeed. In addition to meeting us at the airport, they continued to extend to us their friendship, as well as their valuable time, during this difficult settlement period. For six months, they helped us get settled into life in the new environment—to find accommodations, jobs, schools, grocery stores, doctors and so. They trained us in life skill issues such as budgeting and time-management. We will always be thankful for Australians who reached out then (and now) to the refugee community.

We were the first group of refugees from the South Sudan to settle in Brisbane and within the short time of our arrival a member of our group died. The death caused panic and fear as this was the first death of one of our people in western world culture. The dilemma was that the family of the deceased had no money for a funeral and the South Sudanese community in Brisbane had no resources to facilitate traditional burial or return the body to the homeland. Death back home was accommodated by the community collectively and not by the individual as in Australian culture.

The Sudanese Association approached the Brisbane City Council (BCC) for assistance. The BCC told us that they could help to bury the deceased in a cemetery, but he would be buried in a collective grave along with others. This concept was culturally unacceptable to South Sudanese traditional norms. The leadership of the Association solicited other ethnic groups to donate fifty Australian dollars to collectively pay for the burial. We collected the money and our friend was interred honorably. But the question remained: how do Sudanese/South Sudanese accommodate funerals and burials in Australia or any other western country?

Interacting With Australians

Right from the beginning, we found Australians to be very welcoming to us. I recall a day when we were going to the English classes in the morning with my wife and our youngest son, Anderson, who then was only 18 months old. When we entered the train, it was about 7:30 a.m. In the morning, the trains were packed with many people going to work. We were impressed with Australian's disciplined manner, as they were all quiet. Many were reading a book or a newspaper. Moreover, a young Australian female in her early twenties stood up and offered her seat to my wife, simply because my wife was carrying a baby. Such kind behavior and good manners of this young Queenslander really impressed us. We thought that such exemplary conduct no longer existed in Western cultures. What shocked us was that we had lived in several conservative African countries, towns and cities where such behavior and conduct had already been abandoned.

Another time, I was going to my house at about five o'clock in the evening, and it was raining heavily. An elderly gentleman in his late seventies approached me and asked "Please may I give you a lift to your house?" Of course, I did not hesitate to accept, as I was in need. He drove me to my house. After he dropped me, I said to him, with my African South Sudanese English accent, "Thank you and God bless you." This is a common South Sudanese expression that cannot be missed in such circumstances. Another day I was in the Park Road Station in Brisbane, waiting for a train. Once again it was raining heavily. A woman approached and asked me to share her umbrella. To me, these events were unique and unprecedented, because I was not expecting a liberal Australian Western society to still exhibit such kindly behavior. Well done, Aussies!

One of my friends, an Ethiopian Muslim, was also impressed by how kind and friendly Australians are. He said to me, "Dhano! Why are these Australians doing all these good things so freely for me and my family?" He went on to say "You know, if these Australians become Muslims, they will go to Paradise immediately." I believe this expression of my friend demonstrated how friendly Australians are. Indeed, if not all, the majority of them are.

If a person lives long enough on this planet, you will discover and learn a lot of things. One day, I ordered a taxi and as I was walking to the taxi, with a beautiful South Sudanese smiling face, the taxi driver greeted me and said, "My friend, you are not an Aborigine, are you?" He repeated this same question three times.

"Why?" I asked and he replied, "My friend, that beautiful smiling face is not like an Aboriginal, because an Aboriginal never smiles."

Later I came realize that the taxi driver was probably expressing some of the biases and stereotypes - good and bad - that many Australians have about Aboriginals, a dark-skinned race of people who were indigenous to Australia before British colonization of the continent began in 1788. Later I learned that the

Aboriginals have faced many injustices from the majority population.

Among our group of refugees, I was the first to own a car. I bought a car from Melbourne, Victoria in 1998. It was delivered to my house in Brisbane, Queensland in very good condition, but a couple of days later, the battery failed. The previous owners said "Please purchase a new battery. Send us the receipt, and we will refund the money to you." Once again, I was impressed by the integrity of the Australian people. In 2005, I bought a vehicle from an automobile company in Brisbane, Queensland. With my excellent prior experience with the vehicle company in Melbourne, I neglected to ask for an official vehicle check before signing the purchase document. After a couple of days, I decided to take the car for an inspection. Sadly, I was told that the vehicle "on road cost" should have been only ten thousand dollars. I paid more. So I discovered that, in any society, there are both good people and bad people.

Facing Cultural Challenges

As mentioned earlier, the Sudanese/South Sudanese people are a mixture of ethnicities, religions as well as races, resulting in a rich multicultural and diverse society. During the settlement process, I experienced some aspects of Australian culture that are very different from Sudanese/

South Sudanese culture. I have listed a few of these things in the remainder of this chapter.

Greetings

Greetings are extremely important in Sudan/South Sudanese culture and everyone has time for an extended greeting. A person who does not stop and exchange several greetings is considered unfriendly, impolite or even untrustworthy. Before talking to anyone, it is polite to greet them first. The common greetings vary from community to community. Most of the Sudanese/South Sudanese hug each other, shake hands or wave or raise their right hand (Osterlund, 1978). This would seem extremely excessive to most Australians. Among Australians, handshakes have diminished considerably over the last two generations.

Eye Contact

In most Western cultures, people regard direct eye to eye contact as positive. Australians, for example, teach their children to look a person in the eyes. On the other hand, Sudanese/South Sudanese traditional cultures consider eye contact as a rude or ill-mannered. In Sudan/South Sudan, children are taught to avoid eye contact to show respect. With these different interpretations between Sudanese/ South Sudanese and Australian cultures misinterpretation happens easily.

Socialization

Most Sudanese/South Sudanese are community-oriented. That is, our identity is tied to the group e.g. family or clan. In our communities, people tend to do things collectively, that is, we eat collectively and cultivate collectively. We value collectivity even in decision-making. Like many Western cultures, Australian culture values individualism. They do not easily conform to group values. From an early age, they regard themselves as self-standing persons with their own unique identities. These differences in the socialization process can cause clashes between Australian culture and Sudanese/South Sudanese culture.

Time and Planning

Culturally, it seems that Sudanese/South Sudanese do not plan for tomorrow because they believe that everything relies on God's will. They are spontaneous and flexible in their approach to life. On the other hand, Australians tend to be more structured in their approach to life. They try to plan their day.

In Australian culture, saving time is a value. They enjoy using time efficiently. For them, "time is money." They expect events to begin at the time announced. On the other hand, Sudanese/South Sudanese are not as oriented to the clock as Australians. They do not consider "saving time" as important as experiencing the moment. Thus, in the Sudanese/South Sudanese culture, time is not money or holy, but a cultural practice.

In 1984, a Nuer man passed away in Cairo, Egypt. At that time, I was the Secretary General (SG) of the South Sudanese Students Association (SOSA). So the Sudanese Embassy in Cairo, Egypt asked me to escort the body to Khartoum. I was chosen because I can speak the Nuer language fluently and because of my leadership as the Secretary General (SG) of the South Sudanese Students Association (SOSA). The airline ticket was issued by the Embassy authorities via the Sudan Airways. I was told by Sudan Airways officials to be at the Cairo International Airport by 4:00 p.m. Egyptian time, as the plane would take off at 6:00 p.m. I arrived at exactly 4:00 p.m.—two hours before departure time. However, the plane did not take off until at 6:00 p.m. the following day.

Usually, I travel with the Ethiopian Airlines, which is known all over the African continent for keeping to time schedules and for providing good services. On the other hand, Sudan Airways has taken the nickname of *Inshallah* Airways. This is because when Sudan Airways official inform passengers about the times of flight departures and arrivals, they will always say *Inshallah* ("as God wills"). The Sudan

Airways officials are not as conscious of time and are not as punctual. This illustrates how the culture of a particular people can even extend to management of a corporation.

Hospitality

Both Sudanese and South Sudanese are famous throughout the continent for their hospitality. Hospitality is normally spontaneous. People visit each other without advance invitation. Australians normally expect advance notice of visits and this can be a problem for South Sudanese.

A South Sudanese man worked alongside Australians in an office. One of his workmates lived in the same area and they often carpooled together. As a gesture of politeness, the Australian man said, "Pop in sometimes." A few days later, the South Sudanese went to the Australian's house and rang the doorbell. The Australian opened the door, but he (and his family) seemed very uncomfortable. For Australians hospitality is very important, but it normally requires prior arrangements with the host.

Kinship Relationships

Kinship relationships differ from one culture to another. For example, in most African cultures in general and particularly in the South Sudanese African context, children may have the same father but different mothers. Authentically, South Sudanese say "These are my half-brothers or half-sisters." However, within our cultural context, they are called "sisters" and "brothers."

While in Australia, I sponsored my "niece". Her grandmother is my mother's sister. In the South Sudanese Anyuak culture, I call her my niece. However, the Australian Department of Immigration and Indigenous Affairs (DIMIA) officer said, "She's your cousin." This illustrates differences between the South Sudanese culture and the Australian cultures. Therefore, it is good that the DIMIA considers employing people from African South Sudanese background to assist in such situations.

Names

Among the South Sudanese, the child's ethnic name is associated or connected with actual particulars of the child's life. For example, *Nhial* means "rain" in the Nuer language, and is a common name for baby boys born during rainy season. *Domaac* meaning "bullet" is given to a child born during times of war. South Sudanese who observe Christian beliefs may also carry a Christian name.

Among most, if not at all, ethnic groups in South Sudan, the family name is that of the father or grandfather. Children learn at an early age the importance of their father's lineage. As a result, many Anyuak and Nuer can easily recount at least seven generations of paternal lineage. The perpetuation of the patriarchal names guarantees that children will always be able to trace their ancestry, a key element of South Sudanese culture.

When a Sudanese/South Sudanese family settles in Australia, first, middle and last names are required. Usually, the Nuer and Dinka give their Christian name as their first name followed by their ethnic name as their middle name and their father's name as their last name. But this does vary and can cause problems when registering children in school and so on.

Disability

Disability from the African South Sudanese perspective is viewed as a curse. People regard disability as a punishment because certain ritual sacrifices were not performed for the gods or the ancestors. Therefore, this is the consequence and it is not perceived to be a genetic issue. When such a disability occurs, the family will turn to witchcraft expert for healing. This demonstrates difference in thinking between those South Sudanese who adhere to animistic worldview which is based on the supernatural and the Australian whose worldview is based on science and genetic realities.

Respect for Elderly

Elderly people have great respect in the Sudanese/ South Sudanese community. The elderly people tell the stories orally at night. They relate these stories to the children or young people. Sudanese/South Sudanese are horrified at the idea of Australians' placing their elderly parents in retirement homes.

Death and Burials

Similarities exist along with differences in how the peoples of Sudan and the newly independent Republic of South Sudan perceive death and burial of the dead. The former northern nation is a predominately Sunni Muslim society. At death, they first wash the body, and wrap it with white cloth. According to Muslim tradition, they pray over the body and then take it to the cemetery for burial. Those who bury the dead person must be Muslim, because the Holy Koran/*Quran* or *Hadith*, prophetic tradition says that those who participate in the burial of a Muslim will receive a blessing or reward from Allah. It is a Muslim tradition that a Muslim must be buried in a Muslim cemetery and not be laid to rest in an infidel resting place. The Muslims mourn a dead person for three days, and third day the family of the dead person organizes a feast called in Arabic language *karamah*, which mean honoring, which all the relatives and friends are expected to attend. After forty days, the family of the deceased organizes a big feast called in Arabic language, *arbeen*, which means forty days. Relatives and friends assemble for eating, drinking and prayers.

Among the South Sudanese, there is a mixture of Christianity and African Traditional Religion during funeral and burial ceremonies. In many cases the burial and funeral ceremonies take place on the day after the demise is declared. Certain rituals vary among ethnic groups, but they share most of the same burial customs e.g. digging the grave for burial and wrapping the body with a white cloth or sheets called *damora* or *kaftans*. In accordance with ancient South Sudanese culture, children are not allowed to participate in any burial ceremonies.

The South Sudanese community has three days of mourning for a male and four days for a female. They have the same tradition that, at end of three or four days there will be a feast called to honor the deceased. A bull or ram is slaughtered by relatives and friends as well as the visiting guests who come for prayers. Normally this is done around 3:00 p.m. It is an expensive exercise. As a sign of mourning the women of the family will continue dressing in black clothing for a year. After a year, a final feast is held in honor of the deceased and the women cease wearing black clothing.

Following the arrival of the first generation of South Sudanese refugees in Brisbane, Australia in 1999, the community experienced the passing away of a colleague. This was a big problem for us. As mentioned earlier, most, if not all, Sudanese/South Sudanese societies are community-oriented. That is, we tend to do things collectively. So the family turned to the community for financial help. But at that time, most of us had little or no money. The vast majority of the Sudanese/ South Sudanese were struggling to find employment and relying on social welfare provided by the Australian government's Centre Link. The western culture of insurance and saving money for a funeral is not part of Sudanese/South Sudanese refugee vocabulary. Both Sudanese/South Sudanese tend to do everything on the spot and the increasing expense of burial in the western world had not been a part of their culture. As they become more globalized or assimiliated to life in the western world, issues of death and burial still remain a part of the clash of cultures. The second generation now born and growing up in a new environment will continue to struggle with these issues for years to come.

Neither of the two nations—Sudan/South Sudan—accommodate organ donation or cremation which is taboo in their societies. All view death as the will of God.

65

Eating Habits

The Sudanese/South Sudanese always eat collectively. People usually sit in a circle while eating. Children are given food first before adults. Both the Sudanese and South Sudanese eat their food with the right hand. Using the left hand is a societal taboo.

The Sudanese/South Sudanese in the rural areas have two meals a day, while their counterpart in the urban areas has three meals a day. The breakfast meal is eaten between nine and ten o'clock in the morning. The majority of Sudanese/South Sudanese people have a cup of tea after lunch. The Northern Sudanese are also known to drink strong coffee, which is consumed from a unique tin jug called a *jebena* in Arabic

The Sudanese/South Sudanese community is known to have a sweet tooth. Both communities like sugary desserts. Peanuts are well known and are known as Sudanese beans.

Cultural Foods

The two Sudanese societies, north and south, have been heavily influenced by the Egyptian and Turkish culture during their periods of dominance in Sudan.

The entrance of Arab merchants into Sudan came with a great number of Arabic cultural influences; both in general aspects and particularly on foods such as use of red pepper, garlic, and other spices . They brought with them their "food traditions" like meatballs as well as pastries. These commercial people also taught the Sudanese/South Sudanese to eat fruits and vegetables, which the Sudanese/ South Sudanese community was not familiar in their own cultures.

A most popular food in the two Sudanese communities is sour crepe bread known as *kissera*, which is composed of sorghum and known in Arabic as *dura* or corn. *Kissara* is served with stews, meat, chicken, and fish. The Sudanese/South Sudanese communities rely entirely on meat, fish and milk for their food. Dried fish is popular among Sudanese/South Sudanese people.

Holidays

There were no specific holidays among the Sudanese/South Sudanese communities as there is no calendar in the African traditional culture. However, Christmas and Ramadan Festival are important occasions in the Sudanese/South Sudanese community life.

Muslims worldwide observe Ramadan as a month of fasting. Fasting is required for adult Muslims, except those who are sick, traveling, pregnant, breastfeeding or going through menstrual bleeding. While fasting from dawn until sunset, Muslims refrain from consuming <u>food</u>, drinking liquids, smoking, and <u>abstain from sexual relations</u>. Food and drink is served daily, before sunrise and after sunset. Fasting for Muslims during Ramadan also includes prayers and recitation of the Holy Koran/*Quran*.

During the Muslim fasting month of Ramadan, one of the soft drinks Sudanese Muslims like is known as *hilumur*. It is composed of corn flour and spices.   People also drink *aabrai abiya* which is composed of corn flour like *aabrai.* The two Sudanese Muslim Communities celebrate at the end of the fasting month of Ramadan. They exchange visits among themselves and drink different types of soft drinks while eating cakes and candies.

Pets

In African South Sudanese ethnic groups, particularly in rural areas, pets are an important part of the home life. Dogs are especially to be desired, firstly, because they are useful when men go hunting. Secondly, a dog becomes a reliable guard for the home. At night, with any intrusion the dog will bark. Then the home-owner is prepared, either for a wild animal or an enemy. An Anyuak saying goes "A dog does not bark without reason."

In the urban area, it is very expensive to own and look after a dog. Therefore only wealthy people have pets. In

South Sudan, some cats may be kept as pets, so that the cat will catch and kill any rodents in the house. But keeping a cat in the urban area can also be expensive.

In the Sudan/South Sudan, there are no "pet shops" where a dog or cat may be purchased. It is only when a dog produces puppies, that the puppies may be given free of charge to others.

In the Sudanese/South Sudanese culture, if a snake found in a home, or in the street, is always killed as the snake is a sign of evil. In Australia, the snake may not be killed, but collected by the Animal Protection Agency. When my family came to Australia, we found a snake in the house. I was ready to kill it, but my daughter (Leacha) stopped me. She had learned at school that some people keep snakes as pets. So I consulted our neighbors who made a phone call to the Animal Protection Agency. They came and carried the snake away; the snake was saved to my daughter's satisfaction.

Chapter 5

Clashes in Marriage and Family

Culture is a people's way of life. As shown in the last chapter, the way of life in Australia differs from the way of life in Sudan/South Sudan in many ways. When settling in Australia, Sudanese/South Sudanese face difficult challenges, especially in relation to the sensitive issues of marriage, family relationships, sex education, homosexuality, and so on.

Marriage

Marriage from the African perspective in general, and from the South Sudanese perspective in particular, is an essential part of life that no male or female can avoid culturally and traditionally. If a man or woman reaches the mature age for marriage, they are obliged to marry. If a male has reached a certain age and not married, he is considered an irresponsible fellow. If a female reaches a certain age and is not married, then it is considered that there is something wrong with her or her family. There will be allegations from the community.

From the African South Sudanese perspective, marriage is not for enjoyment of sex. Marriage is for procreation. Traditionally, in some South Sudanese ethnic groups, if not all, children are considered to be the backbone of any marriage. A wife will only really be regarded as married when she has borne a child.

South Sudanese traditional marriage was not between two individuals—a husband and wife—alone, but involved the entire family or clan. Each kin was involved and this provided for its continuance within the community. For these reasons it was not easy for a husband or wife to divorce or separate in those days. Such decisions lie with the relatives and not the husband and wife alone.

Bride Wealth

In most South Sudanese ethnic communities, ownership of cattle is an integral part of their identity. Without cows, their economic, social and spiritual life is not complete. In Dinka and Nuer ethnic communities, cows are very important to their way of life. In marriage, the bride wealth (known as dowry or bride price) embodies the covenant between the two families. Cows or any forms of bride-wealth provide a strong social tie in the South Sudanese community.

From this we can see the significance of a daughter as a source of wealth. The more daughters a father has the richer he becomes and the more respect and prestige he has in the community. Wealth also has connection with the number of sisters a man has. If a male has sisters, he will marry several wives by virtue of his sisters. However, in some tribal communities, for instance Nuer or Dinka (Monjang), if a male has no sisters; his step-brothers have a social obligation to offer a sister to their step-brother.

From the South Sudanese people's point of view, when a daughter is given in marriage, the two families are united. The children of their union become the responsibility of both families, with the major responsibility on the paternal side. In some ethnic groups, like Dinka and Nuer, any brother-in-law will be assisted with some cows to help him build up an *alwak* or herd.

Polygamous Marriages

Polygamous marriages are common in Sudanese/ South Sudanese communities. Both Christian and Muslim marriages are polygamous. Among the Anyuak community, if after a period of time, perhaps five years, a wife has no child, the husband may marry another woman in order that children may be born. If the first wife has been a loyal and dutiful wife, then some of her dowry may remain with her. The husband will take the rest of her dowry with him into the second marriage. Polygamous marriage is illegal in Australia. Here again we can see a clash of two cultures.

Inheritance Marriage

The aim of marriage in African South Sudanese culture is not to satisfy sexual needs or enjoyment, but to produce offspring. That is the core understanding of marriage. Therefore, if a man passes away, one of his closest relatives—brother or cousin—will inherit his wife. If she bears children, these children are considered as offspring of the deceased husband and will bear the decreased husband's name. This is done to keep the name of the deceased alive forever in the family.

In cases of the father's death, the eldest son or uncle automatically inherits his step-mother or his brother's wife according to the Anyuak or some South Sudanese cultures and traditions. However, any children from this union will bear the name of the deceased father even though biologically the children are the son's. Publicly he must acknowledge them only as his brothers or sisters.

Management of Household Finances

Traditionally, the Sudanese/South Sudanese are not adept in financial management. The concept *Inshallah* "as God Wills" is rooted deep in the Sudanese/South Sudanese culture. Their religious belief is that God will provide. Therefore, there is little or no financial planning or budgeting traditionally or culturally; they are not business-minded.

In Sudan/South Sudan, the wages or the salaries are paid monthly, unlike in Australia, where payment usually are fortnightly. Without a budget, the latter is more likely to lead to frivolous spending.

In Sudan/South Sudan the role of the husband is to be the head of the house and the bread winner. As such, the husband is in charge of all income or resources. If the wife earns money herself, traditionally she must give it to the husband who then adds it to his own wages and then allocates the house keeping money to the wife.

Among the South Sudanese, there is a perception that the wife will be a good manager of the household finances. So it is her responsibility to do the shopping and meet all the financial commitments of the household under the authority of her husband. Upon coming to Australia, welfare monies for children (family allowances) from Centre Link (Social Welfare) are given to the wife. This can be the cause of conflicts between husband and wife, or children and parents leading to a breakdown of the family unless a wife is wise enough to handle these monies and still maintain her husband's role as head of the family. Again, this is the clash or dilemma between the two cultures.

Division of Labor

Traditional Sudanese/South Sudanese age and gender roles were different from those in Australia. In Africa, in general, and particularly among the South Sudanese, the division of labor is very clear, defining what men's and women's roles and responsibilities are. The wife's duties are to cook, wash and keep the home clean. She must also look after the children, taking them to the doctor or traditional healer as the need arises. She is also the financial manager and director of household affairs. The husband's duty is to cultivate the land, look after the cattle, and fish. He also provides protection to the family from any danger.

Inheritance and Wills

Traditionally, South Sudanese African families are patriarchal. In the patriarchal family set up, when a father dies, his sons inherit the family's wealth. Normally, the eldest son takes the lion's share of the family's inheritance. The daughters of the family have no entitlement at all. In the tradition, when a bride marries, she leaves her family to live with her husband near or with his parents. Thus daughters are not considered as permanent members of the family, as "tomorrow" they may be married. Until her marriage, her brothers care for her needs.

In the Muslim Sudanese society, the daughter is entitled to a share of the family inheritance. However, with refugees from the South Sudan, Christian or animist, when they come to Australia they face an enormous problem with regard to the inheritance of wealth. Will the girl have a share of the family wealth like her brothers? There are differences between the traditional South Sudanese and the Australian culture. How will the South Sudanese in the diaspora reconcile these differences? I did not have an answer. I leave it for the South Sudanese in Australia as well as elsewhere to resolve this issue. .

Infidelity

In the cultural definition, infidelity occurs whenever a male has sexual intercourse, with another man's wife. This is taken very seriously and in some ethnic groups, infidelity can even cause a death if relatives or authorities do not intervene early.

Normally, infidelity is settled through customary law in a native court, according to tribal norms and rules. The punishment for an adulterous affair varies from one ethnic tribal culture to another. For example, among the Nuer, if a male committed an act of infidelity, he must pay six cows as compensation— known in Nuer language as *ruok*—to the husband's wife. In other ethnic groups, when a man committed infidelity with another man's wife, by tradition he must pay that man compensation in the form of cows or beads or money. There is diversity among the various South Sudanese ethnic groups, so the compensation depends on the culture and tradition of each particular ethnic group.

On the other hand, among the Anyuak and Nuer widow who has commits infidelity is not eligible for infidelity compensation. Why? Because the man who she committed with will not pay compensation and he will not have the right to claim the child. If a child is a girl, he will be entitled to get a cow when the girl is married and it is known in Nuer as *yang ledha* which is literally translated in English as "cow's genitals".

Adultery

From the cultural perspective, adultery is not forbidden per se. A married man or any man has full rights to marry or have sexual intercourse with as many unmarried women he wants. It is a matter of male pride. This is unlike the beliefs of both Christianity and Islam which regard adultery as sin and prohibit sex outside of marriage. Outside the bonds of marriage, sex is not considered sinful, according to the African traditional religion. This is why the HIV/AIDS epidemic was able to spread and has become a social and economic headache to African political leadership, as well as to civil society.

Obviously, adultery/infidelity cause some threat to the steadiness of marriage, as well as to the general security of the public. It should be noted that the impact of twenty-one year of war in the South Sudan has introduced some social ills such as prostitution and HIV/AIDS due to the collapse of traditional family values. The resultant stress and anxiety within the families is a matter of concern in South Sudan, and is an even greater matter of concern among diaspora families in Australia. Suspicion and lack of trust have arisen among families, relatives and the wider South Sudanese community.

Incest

The Sudanese Northern Arabs may marry within the same kinship. But in the African South Sudanese African community, it is taboo for any male or female having a blood relationship to have sexual intercourse. It is regarded as incest. In this case, a ritual sacrifice is performed to avoid any curse upon the two people concerned.

In African South Sudanese culture, there is also a perception that if a man has sexual relations with two women, who are blood-related to each other, both will die. Traditionally, parents teach their children the rules regarding sex especially with regard to infidelity e.g. having affairs with those who related to them or with the wives of others. Obviously, these are extremely serious matters as death will most likely be the end result.

However, if a man's wife dies without having borne him any children, by the Anyuak tradition and custom, he is allowed to take his sister-in-law as a wife. In the case where there are children, the husband is also allowed to take his sister in-law as a wife, because it is considered that she will care for the children more properly.

Paternity vs Child Support

When a young male conceives a girl, the parent or relative of the male must pay the compensation cost. Again it depends on customary laws and norms of each ethnic group. Among most of the Nilotic groups, like Shilluk (Collo), the punishment can vary between four to six cows, to be given to girl's parents. It is known in Collo culture as a *kour*, which literally means "blood dowry". In Nuer culture, if a child is a girl, the boy's family pays six cows. If the child is a boy, it is compensated with four cows only. When the compensation is paid, that is the end of the affair. This is not like child support which continues until the child is eighteen years old in Australia and some other Western cultures.

Sex Education

In South Sudan, sex education is not taught in schools or spoken about in the home. It is considered as a taboo for parents to talk about sex with their children. So the children must learn about sex naturally or from their peer groups. When South Sudanese children come to Australia, where sex is openly discussed, this causes conflict between the two cultures, and becomes a dilemma for South Sudanese parents. Again we see the clash of two cultures.

Traditionally, in the African South Sudanese culture, girls were not allowed to have a "boyfriend," or to recognize any male as such. In Australia, girls and boys both bring "boyfriends" or "girlfriends" openly into the home. The concept is difficult for South Sudanese parents to comprehend. In Australia, some South Sudanese families allow flexibility for their boys to socialize at a reasonable age, whereas the restrictions formerly applied still confine the girl in the family as a vulnerable person.

Homosexuality

The practice and perception of homosexuality is a foreign and bizarre concept in African traditional culture and especially in South Sudan. However, in the Northern Sudan Arabized/Muslim culture the concept of homosexuality is not bizarre at all. When South Sudanese started going to the

North Sudan in the 1950s, they discovered open practice of homosexuality in houses of prostitution. In those days, most of the South Sudanese were domestic workers.

The Arabic language of North Sudan provides verification that the concept of homosexuality is not unusual. We can find that the specific words for homosexual relationships are available in Sudan Arabic language. For example, in classical Arabic the homosexual male who acts as a female within the homosexual relationship is termed *lutiyy* (singular), *lutiaa* in plural. The one who acts as male within the homosexual relationship is called *khwoll* in classical Arabic. Nonetheless, in Sudan as an Islamic/Arab state, the open practice of homosexuality is a taboo, although it is practiced secretly.

In South Sudan the concept of homosexuality is entirely, taboo, totally unaccepted in the community, and illegal by the laws of the land. If a person is discovered as a homosexual in South Sudan, that individual will be isolated if not murdered by the family or relatives. The word "homosexual" is not available in most, if not all, the South Sudanese languages. Thus, somebody somewhere may post a question why this South Sudanese author is writing about this taboo social issue. I have three reasons.

First, I want to prepare my colleagues in the Diaspora as parents to face reality. The South Sudanese now live in Australia, USA, and Canada, etc. Their children spend eight hours daily in school or somewhere with peers or friends. The South Sudanese youth in the Diaspora do not live on their own island. They live within the Western world culture and life style. Therefore, the South Sudanese parent should not be surprised to someday hear a declaration from their child "Dad and Mum, I'm gay" or "Dad and Mum, I'm a lesbian." What will be the response of the parents toward their child? As a matter of fact, I have unconfirmed sources that, there is one South Sudanese boy in Midwest, USA who has already declared himself as openly gay. Homosexuality is going to be reality with parents in the Diaspora. Thus, parents need to have courage and face the issue with wisdom or there will be an inevitable clash of two cultures and a generation culture gap.

Secondly, we must educate our GOSS that we live in a globalized era. What takes place in Australia, USA, and Canada, etc. will eventually have an impact on South Sudanese people. For example, the US President Barak Obama and his former Secretary of State Hilary Clinton have enshrined in American foreign policy the issue of gay and lesbian rights. This issue is connected with the any technical aid given to any government. It may be that the rest of the Western governments will follow suit soon. What will be response of the South Sudan government and other African governments? The South African Government has a first ever liberal constitution on the continent.

Third, I want to educate our friends who are gay or lesbian who may think of visiting the South Sudan that South Sudan is a conservative society and they should exercise wisdom when talking about their sexuality. Sexuality is not discussed openly in South Sudan and homosexuality is taboo as well as illegal by the laws of the land.

The Laws of the Republic of South Sudan – or in other words the Transitional Constitution, 2011 Part Two – Bill of Rights under the Right of Found a Family: "**Every person of marriageable age shall have the right to marry a person of the opposite sex and to found a family according to their respective family laws, and no marriage shall be entered into without the free and full consent of the man and woman intending**" pg 6. From this quotation of the South Sudan Transitional Constitution 2011, it is loud and clear that same sex marriage is absolutely illegal in the RSS.

It should be noted that sodomy or sodomizing a boy in Sudan or in some, if not all Arab/Islamic states, does not carry a severe punishment whereas sexual intercourse with a woman or girl carries a grave or severe punishment by stoning because it is considered as a shame by the Arab/ Islamic culture. In some Islamic countries, honor killings are directed mostly against women and girls due to some known or perceived shame and it is not regarded as murder. However, honor killings of a woman or wife is not common in Sudanese/South Sudanese society.

Female Genital Mutilation (FGM)

The Female Genital Mutilation (FGM) well known as a female circumcision refers to the partial cutting of the partial or entire removal of female clitoris? The traditional culture concept behind the circumcision of a girl or a woman among the Arabized Northern Sudanese Muslim Community was to reduce the girl's or woman's desire or lust for sex. The performing of the FGM carries different components of the traditional socio-cultural and religious meaning respectively.

The Arabized Northern Muslim Sudanese Community has been practicing the FGM for girls at the age of 13 years old and above. The Arabized Northerners Sudanese Muslim community practiced two types of the female circumcision namely:

1. Pharaonic circumcision: Which mean the complete removal of the clitoris and known in Arabic language as *katan phorone*

2. Sunni circumcision: Which mean cutting partial of clitoris and known in Arabic language as *katan sunni*

FGM is practiced across the globe, but it has mainly been performed on two continents, namely Africa and Asia. The US State Department has recognized fourteen African countries where the FGM are widely performed, and of course Sudan is one of those countries. The prevalence of FGM is estimated to be 91% in Sudan. Since the Islamic government came to power in Khartoum in 1989, it has been campaigning vigorously against this bad practice and raising the theme that the circumcision of girls and women is an un-Islamic practice.

Because of the immigration of African refugees, the traditional FGM practice has extended to Australia; the practice of the FGM has bad medical and sexual consequences and sexual impact on girls as well as women.

How to Overcome FGM

In 1997, formal research was done by the World Health Organization (WHO) on the severe health consequences of FGM, mainly practiced on the African continent. In 1999, the First Lady of Nigeria became the spokesperson for the campaign against the practice of FGM and launched it to international attention. Other African First Ladies also organized campaigns against this horrible practice of FGM. Grassroots campaigns were started in Chad, Sudan, and Central African Republics to work exclusively on eradication of female genital mutilation. The United Nations has declared 6th February as the International Day of Zero Tolerance to Female Genital Mutilation and called for stronger collaboration in African countries on the campaign against female genital mutilation. Since then, anti-FGM campaigns have been initiated around the world.

I strongly believe that the stakeholders in Australia such as the Multicultural Development Association (MDA) and Queensland Torture & Trauma Community Association (QTTCA) around Australia and others can work together in partnership to minimize this inhumane traditional practice. The three arms of the governments namely—the Federal, State and Municipal governments—can be mobilized to raise funds for conferences, seminars and workshops. These conferences will be geared toward education and enlightenment of both gender—female and male Sudanese in particular and African communities in general to minimize this unacceptable cultural practice. Women associations need to be involved because they are the venerable groups.

I believe we have the power to change the culture of our Sudanese/South Sudanese community in Australia. We need women and men with common sense who will not galvanize the bad caused by the practice of FGM, but will work to prevent the further practice of FGM. The press and the media also can play an active role in education enlighten among the Sudanese Australian community in particular and the African Australian community in general. We need to work hard together to disseminate the message against FGM - social, moral and spiritual teaching so as to avoid further violence against the mothers and leaders of tomorrow.

All of us, the Sudanese/South Sudanese community in Australia and the Australian stakeholders who are involved with the refugees and immigrants are part of the problem albeit indirectly. We all need to be involved in seeking a solution. No one can condone this despicable practice of the FGM against our girls and women. We must save our daughters and sisters and benefit all humanity for that matter.

Chapter 6

Our Community in Queensland

Due to religious persecution in the 1980s, Sudanese Coptics were the first group to arrive in Australia, especially in Brisbane, Queensland. The first South Sudanese refugees group arrived in Brisbane, Queensland in 1996. Most of them came to Australia as political refugees. A great number of South Sudanese refugees came from Cairo, Egypt and from Kenya, Ethiopia and Uganda. DIMA (Department of Immigration and Multicultural Affairs) estimated from 1st January 1990 to 30th June 1999, there were 97 females and 124 males, the total number of immigrants from South Sudan being 221 adults and children (DIMA-Data 1999). Today, of course, the number is larger than the above-mentioned figures.

The Sudanese/South Sudanese community are scattered around Queensland. However, the largest number of them live in the Brisbane area especially on the southern side of the city of Brisbane, namely Yeronga, Moorooka, Yerongapilly and Sunnybank. The Queensland/South Sudanese community is comprised of a variety of ethnic groups. The majority of them come from the Dinka, Bari and Nuer communities plus other small communities.

Community Politics

The historical establishment of the Sudanese Community of Queensland goes back to December 1997. It came as a result of the Sudanese people who had come to Brisbane, Queensland, in the late 1990s. The first presidency was given to Mr. Mojo Shallei from Nubia Mountains.

In 1996 the influx of South Sudanese caused a small increase in the numbers living in Brisbane. Over the next two years, the numbers were gradually, but steadily increasing. By 1998, the South Sudanese number jumped almost 100 percent. That led them to seek for change in leadership and in the Management Committee of the Sudanese Association of Queensland Incorporated (SAQIN). People commenced meeting in individual houses, consulting among themselves, as to who would lead the people in this new era. The selection went to two men namely Mr. Gabriel Okuno, of Western Bahar-al-Gahazal State, a graduate of a Libyan University who has studied Bachelor Degree in Political Sciences. The second man was Mr. Alison Delia from Central Equatoria State, a graduate of the Agriculture Institute in the South Sudan. After thorough discussion among members, Mr. Okuno stepped down in favor of Mr. Delia. Prior to that, it was decided that each person nominated should be nominated by one member and seconded by a different person.

This author nominated Mr. Delia, and this nomination was seconded by another person. Mr. Delia was challenged for the top job by the competent and experienced Dr. Magdei Al Abumagedi, Ph.D. Northern Sudanese Arab/ Muslim. Due to previous consultation and lobby on the election procedure, the election took just thirty minutes. It was a normal democratic practice and procedure without any conspiracy against any group.

In 2000 there were three main Sudanese Associations in Brisbane, Queensland: namely the Chapter/ the political wing of the Sudan People's Liberation Movement (SPLM) Incorporated, and the Sudanese Association of Queensland Incorporated (SAQIN), and the Sudanese Christian Fellowship of Queensland Incorporated (SCFQIN). Around that time, the Northern Arabized Muslim and Sudanese Arab Coptics disappeared from community politics. I do not know why they were no longer active in the Sudanese Community.

More cultural clashes occurred as the South Sudanese Community organized and encountered bureaucratic structures in the host country. I have discussed a few of these things in the remainder of this chapter.

Policing Service

The history of the establishment of the Police Force goes back to the colonial era. The Sudanese pioneer police came up with a beautiful slogan for the police service. Literally translated, it means "A clean hand and an eye that cannot sleep all night." Another slogan says "The Police are under the People's Service." Thus, if something happen anywhere and at any time, any citizens is entitled to call the police to rescue them and the police are obliged to respond without hesitation and without going deeply into details or questions. Immediate assistance is given, and proper investigations are conducted later on. This is the Sudanese/ South Sudanese policing service culture. They do not need to wait for hard evidence as the Australian Police service culture may demand.

When I interviewed some South Sudanese in Brisbane, Australia, about the policing culture in Brisbane, one man told me that another man had an affair with his wife. He reported the case to the police several times. However, the police did not take him seriously. The police said that he needed to bring hard evidence, like a photograph, a video or a witness to the adulterous affair.

Although he had reported his case several times to the police, the police continued to ignore him. Eventually, the husband was so frustrated with the Australian police that he took the law into his own hands. The police arrested him when he attempted to kill the adulterer. He went on to tell me, "The good thing with the Australian police is that they will stop you if you have committed an offense."

In the Sudanese/South Sudanese culture, when a person reports a case to the police, it is taken seriously, especially a wife's affair. As mentioned in an earlier chapter, culturally and traditionally, in most South Sudanese ethnic groups, if a wife has affairs with another man, it is an insult to her husband, and most of the time, it will lead to a death. So the Sudanese/South Sudanese police take everything seriously even unfounded accusations. The proof comes later!

In another interview a married woman told me that she was frustrated with the Australian police due to their discriminatory behavior. She explained that her husband beat her mercilessly. She phoned the police three times, but they did not come to her rescue. "When my neighbors heard my screaming," she said. "It seems they called the police. Eventually the police came, but it was already too late and I was bleeding. So I chased them away." She added, "When a call is made to the police, and the caller has a foreign accent, the call is ignored, or the situation is not taken seriously' unless there is a death." Apparently, this is often the case. On the other hand, some parents mentioned that when the South Sudanese children call police everywhere and anytime in Australia, the police arrive without delay.

Again it becomes problematic when children call the police against parental discipline. In most Sudanese/South Sudanese cultures, parents (and other elders within the community) are expected to discipline children and corporal punishment (spanking or whipping) is common when children misbehave. However, children in the Diaspora have been known to call the police claiming child abuse after being spanked and the parents were arrested. Living in Australia has changed traditional authority relationships and caused conflict within Sudanese/South Sudanese families and communities.

These comments are not intended as an indictment of the Australian police system. My observation is that there is not too much difference between the Sudanese and the Australian police systems, in terms of written laws or regulations. The only differences I can observe are that the Australian police system adheres strictly to the principles of democratic process, good governance, human rights and execution of written laws and regulations. In contrast, the police in the Sudan/South Sudan do not. Sudanese/South Sudanese have no right to form a trade union (as is the case in Australia) because the police force in Sudan/South Sudan is considered as a part of the organized forces like the army. However, with these different policing culture issues, it is clear that the role of the ethnic Police Liaison Officer (PLO) should be to educate both parties, the Australian police service as well as the Sudanese/South Sudanese community with regards to the policing culture challenges and differences.

Centre Link: A Blessing or a Curse?

Centre Link is an arm of the Australian government that delivers services to assist people in need to become self-sufficient. In the Sudan/South Sudan culture, the husband is the bread winner and the wife is entirely reliant upon him since in most African countries, there is no social welfare/social security system. Traditionally, in South Sudan the husband is head of the household. The wife is the symbol of unity, stability and peace of the family. So when the husband and wife are functioning in their traditional roles, then the family is at peace. However, in Australia, refugees are eligible for assistance from Centre Link, given as "family assistance and parenting allowance." These monies from Centre Link are given to the wife. This has been the cause of separation or divorce in some families, as a result of the Sudanese/ South Sudanese wife becoming economically independent or empowered.

Workforce Experience

The Sudanese/South Sudanese in general are viewed by many people as the laziest people on earth. The modern Arabized Northern Sudanese also consider the South Sudanese as the laziest people in Sudan failing to acknowledge that the South Sudanese are the ones who constructed the buildings in the whole of Northern Sudan. Nevertheless, my experience as a settlement worker for both the Red Cross of Queensland and the Multicultural Development Association (MDA) for nearly five years working with Sudanese/South Sudanese groups in particular and African groups in general, has proved that these allegations are false.

Their work experience with the Australian Meat and Poultry Factories just to give an example has validated that the Sudanese/South Sudanese are very hard working people. To confirm this, during my work experience, I received several telephone calls from various Meat and Poultry Factories as well as other companies requesting me to recommend some Sudanese/South Sudanese to work for them.

In actuality, laziness is regarded as a bad habit in the Sudanese/South Sudanese culture and custom. If it so happens that a person is not a hard worker, then he or she will not be accepted in society. However, there are direct or indirect reasons that do not make the Sudanese/South Sudanese working experience back home motivating or attractive. These three major factors are as following:-

1. **Wages or salaries are not paid on time**. In the Western world an employee gets her or his wages and salaries on time whether fortnightly or monthly without delay from the government or private sector. These factors alone motivate people to work hard.

2. **Lack of accountability, answerability and responsibility if employee is late or absent from work**. In the Western world in general and especially in Australia an employee is held accountable and answerable for their absences. Being late or absent may lead to immediate dismissal and the employee will not find it easy to get another job. In Sudanese/South Sudanese culture such a culture of accountability and answerability is not there. Unfortunately if the bosses

become harder on workers, they will hate the bosses or make a lot of allegations against them.

3. **No motivation or attractive mechanisms or factors in place for institutions like in the public sector**. However, when a Sudanese/South Sudanese working in overseas, they demonstrate that they are hardworking people, devoted to sustain their families and extended families.

Language Acquisition

The refugees and migrants who came to Australia and settled in the 1990s experienced a struggle as their children became bilingual while parents struggled to preserve their mother tongue. In most cases, Sudanese/ South Sudanese parents want their children to know their mother tongue. But the children spend eight hours per day in school and child care and quickly pick up English language usage exceeding their parents and become interpreters and translators for the parents. Unfortunately they lose their mother tongue because it is limited to home use among the family. When the children are playing alone, they speak English and hear it when watching television. These factors accelerate loss of the mother tongue.

The dilemma of language acquisition is an essential element in preserving the culture and identity of any group in the Diaspora. The Australian Commonwealth government endorsed a policy of multiculturalism as a way forward to promote refugees and migrants in their cultures and languages within the context of Australian society. Settlement of the refugee community was government policy for boosting population and promoting multiculturalism in Australian society.

This dilemma is an important element in the clash of cultures. The question becomes how to minimize the loss of mother tongue usage. It behooves the Australian and state governments to assist the South Sudanese refugees and migrants with resource centers for Saturday sessions where instruction in the mother tongue language can promote the multiculturalism policy and preserve their culture, customs, and language.

Culture of Silence

Breaking of the "culture of silence" in the South Sudanese community in Brisbane, or indeed elsewhere in Australia, must also be addressed. The South Sudanese community in Australia needs to restore a sense of self-confidence and self-esteem. This will not happen overnight, but will take time because the "culture of silence" is a part of

99

South Sudanese tribal culture. The South Sudanese community members come from a conservative cultural background and an authoritarian regime, where there has not been any practice of democratic values.

It is possible to observe in any meeting even though things are not on the right track, there will be silence. This is because, back in Sudan/South Sudan, if people voiced their opinions, the Security or Police authorities might follow them and arrest them. Thus, if any service provider comes up with a project proposal, it is not questioned. Not because the Sudanese/South Sudanese community likes it, but because people are afraid to speak up. And silence may mean acceptance or rejection.

On the other hand, some South Sudanese may at times be very vocal, and when it comes to community politics some of them, if not all, may be ambitious. Ambitious itself, is not a negative thing, as long as it is matched with ability and competency.

Utilizing Partnerships

The population of South Sudanese Diaspora in the USA alone is estimated to be 90,000 to 100,000 according to a 2010 estimate of community leaders.   There are an estimated 30,000 to 35,000 South Sudanese in Canada and South Sudanese in the Diaspora in Australia are estimated at

31,000. I can conservatively estimate that there are 300,000 to 500,000 South Sudanese Diaspora worldwide.

In this 21st century, the exodus of people across international borders makes an important impact especially when the strengths of the component parties are human and economic assets. My observation is that diaspora communities have two main partners: the host country and the home country. These two form a potentially stronger whole, when utilizing the strengths of both partners. As a result, the diaspoa community will be strengthened and the diaspoa community will be empowered to strengthen both the host country (Australia) and home country (our beloved South Sudan).

The American Agency for International Development reports the following activities for these communities

- Advocacy and public diplomacy
- Volunteerism
- Philanthropy
- Trade and tourist
- Investment in activities in country of origin capital markets.
- Investment by diaspora entrepreneurs

Source: (USAID – Diaspora / New Partners in Global Development Policy)

To build the capability of our diaspora communities overseas, I   advocate that, we need to empower our embassies financially in   building and strengthening the capability of our diaspora community in service centers for training in the areas of project proposals, accounting duties and funds financial management and investment laws in South Sudan. I also   recommend that the GOSS establish a commission to oversee our diaspora communities as well as articulate policies related to diaspora communities   under the proposed name: Diasporas, Migrants and Expatriates Commission (DMEC) with branches in our ten states, plus we enshrine it in our foreign policy.

As Africa's newest nation, the Government of South Sudan needs   to learn from   all countries hosting our Diaspora. We need to learn lessons about diaspora administration and experiences. It is my hope that our South Sudanese diaspora will play an active role in the growth of our beloved country by contribution   of ideas, knowledge, and skills. I also   hope the Government of South Sudan will ensure that the Diaspora communities and the embassies in countries overseas participate in collecting information and creating a database about the Diaspora, migrants and expatriates in their respective countries.

Chapter 7

The Anyuak Kingdom: Yesterday and Today

The Anyuak nationality is one member of the Luo nationality group. The Luo nationalities in the South Sudan are Collo (Shilluk), Achoi, Pari, Blamda-Bor, Chad, Anyuak and Luo (known as Jurchol). Dr. Conradin Perner known in Anyuak Kingdom as *Kwacakworo* (which means tiger-leopard in Anyuak) has noted in his book that the Anyuak Kingdom originated from Rumbek in the Lakes State area. According to the Anyuak oral tradition, Gilo who was the grandfather of the Anyuak Kingdom, had two brothers namely, Dimo who is the grandfather of the Luo of the Western Bahr al-Ghazal (Jur), and the second brother was Nyikango the grandfather of the Collo Kingdom (Shilluk).Gilo was the elder brother to both Dimo and Nykiango.

As a consequence of a dispute over the issue of *Dimu* (precious bead) which was swallowed by his daughter, every one of the three brothers went on his own way. The Nyikango Kingdom settled in the Sobat River mouth and along the White Nile, while Dimo proceeded to the current Wau town area. Also the Gilo continued their journey along the Sobat River toward east and finally they settled in Nyium which is currently eastern Jikang Nuer area (Nasir). In the 1880s, the

Nuer and the Anyuak Kingdom over ran several vicinities including Okadi Vicinity.

In the twentieth century the *Nyiya* (king) namely Odiel Wa Kuat and Oliimi Wa Aganya disputed with Jikany Nuer, but unfortunately the two *Nyiyas* were unsuccessful to vanquish Nuer. Oshwak or the Royal emblems which were considered by the Anyuak Kingdom as political tokens became the essential factor in the Anyuak Kingdom's big horrifying disagreement.

His Majesty *Nyiya* Akwei War Cham was the one who controlled the Royal emblems (*Ochwak*) of the Anyuak Kingdom in 1910. Plus, he was the *Nyiya* of Adongo Anyuak sub-clan. In 1920, His Majesty *Nyiya* Akwei War Cham went back to the river, an Anyuak expression, meaning he died. After his death Mr. Lieutenant Colonel Bacon managed to visit Adongo (Pochall County) Anyuak sub-clan vicinity, after the British District Commissioner (DC) was absent from the Pochalla District for fourteen years.

Having been neighbors for many generations, the Anyuak and Nuer communities are old traditional enemies even though they have intermarriage between them.

In 1920 when the Anglo-Ethiopians demarcated the international borders, the small rivers became the artificial border dividing the so-called South Sudanese Anyuak and

Ethiopian Anyuak on the other side. With the so-called demarcation of international borders, the Anyuak Kingdom was the most immediately contrived being divided by illegal and unfair administrative frontier into two groups namely so-called Ethiopian Anyuak and South Sudanese Anyuak respectively.

The essential token of governmental loyalty of the Anyuak Kingdom were the royal emblems of heir looms, which are composed of the spears, iron, two thrones (the tooth drum and most importantly the five necklaces).The royal emblems or heir looms was instituted by Ocotho Wa Jwonim according to the Anyuak oral traditional.

In 1912, The Anglo-Egyptian administration came aware of the aristocracy which has led by His Majesty *Nyiya* (King) Akwei War Cham the grandfather of the current His Majesty *Nyiya* Akwei Agada Akwei, and it was inherited by his son prince Cham Wa Akwei who was only twelve years old when he was installed as *Nyiya*. The Anyuak Kingdoms are inherited by claimant male progeny. Ottlo village is the headquarters of the royal Anyuak Kingdom in Pochalla County, Jonglei State.

His Majesty *Nyiya* Agwa War Akwon was the last enthroned holder of the royal emblems, and the British D.C. in Akobo commenced to give him salary of one Sudanese pound per month as a part of establishment of the Anyuak of Openo Anyuak clansmen. Gambella town for the GOS was a lifeline for generating custom revenue for the Ministry of Finance in Khartoum, Sudan in those days.

In 1920, the sizeable number of Ethiopians from the highland came to Gambella and was shifted from the Customs Department to the Upper Nile Province administration and leadership.

In 1930, the Emperor Haile Selassie became the Emperor of the whole Ethiopia including the isolated borders. In 1942, His Majesty the late Agda Wa Akwei was installed as a *Nyiya* at age of 20. He reigned over 58 years. His Majesty Nyiya Agda Wa Akwei was working as a messenger at Akobo district where he was brought from.

His Majesty Nyiya Agada Wa Akwei during his stay and work in Akobo married his first wife (Queen Aguot), and they were blessed with offspring. Their son was the late prince John Adongo Agada. His Majesty the late *Nyiya* Adongo Akwei Agada Akwei was installed as a *Nyiya* in March 2001, when his father H.M. Nyenya Agada Akwei Cham passed away in 2000. When his father passed away, he was a refugee in Canada, from Canada he went back home and become a *nyiya* (king).

According to his father's *legnii* (will), Prince Adongo Agada was to replace him, followed by Prince Adosh Agda and then Prince Akwei Agada Akwei who was by then living in USA and the current *nyiya*. According to sources close to the late His Majesty Nyiya Agada Akwei Cham, the reason he named his three sons publicly was to avoid any kind of controversy among his children by the Adongo Anyuak clan, that is, to avoid any dispute or rivalry in the future.

In 2001 Prince Adongo Agada was installed as a *nyiya* of Oshwok. Late *Nyiya* Adongo Agada was chosen among hundreds if not thousands of male children.

On 25th April 2012 the Anyuak Kingdom in Adongo region installed Prince Akwei Agada Akwei as *Nyiya* of Oshwok and His Majesty Akwei Agada Akei become the 24th *Nyiya* of the Adongo Anyuak Kingdom. The Anyuak Kingdom emblem is formed of the Crown, the *Dimu*, the Lion, the Leopard, the Shield and Spear, and the Hoe. It is worth noting here that His Majesty *Nyiya* Akwei Agad Akwei succeeded his brother late His Majesty *Nyiya* Adongo Agada Akwei who passed away on 30th November 2011 in Nairobi, Kenya.

History of the Akobo District (County)

According to my father's legend the Akobo District was moved from Akobo Gedem in Arabic (Old Akobo) in 1910, because Akobo Gedem faced floods every year, the

109

British District Commissioner (DC) recommended that Akobo be moved to its current location. Akobo District came out as part of Pibor River Province, and after some time the name was altered to Sobat Pibor District. In 1925 the Akobo District was annexed to be a part of the Civil Administration of Upper Nile Province. The Akobo District ruled two communities namely, Anyuak-Ciro clan and Murle, respectively. The Nuer inhabitants west of the Bahr-el Jebel were not under any province for almost 20 years. In 1913, the British Administration came up with the idea to combine most of Western Nuer in the civil rule of the Zeraf Valley District. Mr. Tunnicliffe spoke the Anyuak language.

In 1931, the British Administration reckoned that the Ciro-Anyuak clan of Akobo District was 25,000, the rest stayed inside the Ethiopian boundary. The Anyuak Kingdom (inhabitants of Akobo District) was split into two clans, namely the Akobo-Ciro Anyuak clan (Chieftain System) and the Pochalla Adongo-Anyuak clan (Kingdom). The District Commissioner did not visit the Pochalla region of Adongo clan until 1922 when the military ruler came to Otalo Village, and he endorsed rotating of the Monarch by His Majesty *Nyiya* Cham Akwei, son of His Majesty *Nyiya* Akwei Cham the ruler of Anyuak guard, on the basis that His Majesty *Nyiya* Cham Akwei had inherited Nyiya.

In 1931, according to the Upper Nile Province Handbook Report there were four Lou-Nuer-Mor vicinities, and the vicinities were Dengjok village and his Chief was Chief Faragalla Kong, Kana Village was headed by Chief Koryom Kom, Meir vicinity was headed by Chief Nyang Camjok and Koingai was headed by Chief Deng Rue. All four vicinities are part of the Akobo District. Lou-Nuer-Mor was evaluated on equal ground as the Ciro-Anyuak people. Beside four Lou-Nuer-Mor clans, there was Kaibui village which was headed by Chief Pec Ruac who first lived in Kaikwi and Kurwai and migrated to Kaibui. Kaibui belong to Lou-Nuer-Mor clan of Lual Tiang, who was succeeded by his son, Paramount Chief, the late Mr. Gang Lual Tiang, who was working closely with the Paramount Chief of Ciro-Anyuak the late Mr. Otheri Jok. All these Lou-Mor-Nuer villages lived in Ciro-Anyuak territory according to the British colonial Administration boundaries of first of January 1956. According to the Upper Nile Report in 1931, the Lou-Nuer-Mor people were constrained from fishing. However, in 1926, the District Commissioners held a conference, when sub-clan of Lou-Nuer-Mor was called to allow to grazing of their cows during the dry season at Beim. The Lou-Nuer-Mor tribe was not accepted to build in the area.

Two Anyuak and two Murle worked as interpreters. Mr. Omot Giba had worked as an interpreter for ten years and Mr. Odol Owar had been employed for two years. The two Murle who were employed as interpreters for Murle community in Akobo District were Mr. Lokadi and Mr. Jakor. All four Anyuak and Murle were officially employed by the Akobo District local government. His Majesty *Nyiya* Akwei-Wor-Cam (Chan) took the Anyuak Kingdom emblems from his cousin His Majesty *Nyiya* Uliimi-Wor-Aganya. His Majesty *Nyiya* Akwei-Wor-Cham passed away in October 1920, and he had handed over the Anyuak Kingdom emblems to his twelve year old son named Prince Cam-Wor-Akwei who reigned from 1908-1933. However, His Majesty *Nyiya* Cam-Wor-Meditto did not recognize His Majesty *Nyiya* Cam-Wor-Akwei as *Nyiya*. By 1922 Lt. Colonel Bacon arrived in Otalo village (now Payam), the headquarters of the Anyuak Kingdom. In 1921 Lt. Colonel Bacon the DC endorsed Prince Cam as *nyiya* (king). The Anyuak Kingdom was divided between Sudan and Ethiopia in 1921. An accusation was brought against His Majesty *Nyiya* Cam-Wor-Akwei by another Anyuak *Nyiya* (King) led His Majesty *Nyiya* Cam-Wor-Akwei to imprisonment as well as deposition in 1927. Between1928-1933 he repeatedly escaped to Ethiopia to evade the tribunal situation in the Sudan. Mr. Ochodo was the immediate ancestor of the Anyuak Kingdom, where the monarch originated from. The Anyuak tribal administration system is based in Adongo Anyuak clan, and is ruled by *nyiya* (king). While the Ciro-Anyuak of Akobo administrative system was based on the chieftain. It is based on the rank of *kwaaro* (single chief) *kwari* (plural chiefs).

The Anyuak Kingdom and Shilluk (Collo) Kingdom have some similarities and some differences as well. The Collo Kingdom have only sole central *reth* (king), while the Anyuak Kingdom has many nobles or *nyiya* (kings), and these *nyiya* are completely independent administratively, politically and economically. However, the Anyuak Kingdom recognized the most senior *nyiya* as the one who holds the royal emblems, which are based in the Otalo village. Currently, the most senior *nyiya* is His Majesty *Nyiya* Akwei Wor-Agada who was installed as a *nyiya* on April 25, 2012, and His Majesty *Nyiya* Akwei becomes 24th *nyiya* of the Anyuak Kingdom in line since the establishment of the Anyuak Kingdom by Ochodo.

The Anyuak Kingdom *nyiya* has no direct political influence. Because, as soon as he meddles in political affairs that will cause conflict of interest, and it means that he becomes biased and he will lose his respect and credibility in the Anyuak Kingdom. The Anyuak Kingdom is represented in the Diaspora by the Anyuak Kingdom of South Sudanese in the Diaspora (AKSSD), however it has a branch in Australia and its membership is composed of two counties, namely, Akobo County (Ciro Clan) and Pochalla County (Adongo Clan).

Recent Akobo Political History

In 1980, the general election was conducted in the Southern Sudan region by then. In this election, Professor Paul Andei Othow (Ciro-Anyuak) candidate contested with Dr. Michael Wall Dunny and Justice John Luk Jok (both Lou-Nuer-Mor) candidates. Prof. Paul Andei Othow won the People's Regional Assembly seat of Akobo District constituency. As a result of Prof. Paul Andei Othow winning the seat, the conflict between the two communities intensified. After three years, exactly in April of 1983, the elites and intelligentsia of Lou-Mor-Nuer organized a conspiracy against the Ciro-Anyuak community inside Akobo town and by broad daylight massacred more than one hundred Ciro-Anyuak clan people, among them were the author's father who was killed praying after the noon Muslim prayers. Those of Lou-Mor-Nuer elites and intelligentsia were not brought to justice by Mr. Abel Aler, the Vice President of the Republic of Sudan and the President of the High Executive Council of the Regional Government of the day. However, I would like to say that, I have forgiven those who killed my dear Dad. *God forgive them for they knew not what they were doing.*

Reconciliation between Ciro-Anyuak and Lou-Nuer-Mor What is the way forward?

The way forward is to engage the two communities to dialogue and discuss solutions to the problem. Akobo County traditionally and historically belongs to the Ciro-Anyuak clan. However, Lou-Nuer-Mor settled in Akobo nearly four decades ago and the two communities have inter-married amongst themselves.

Therefore, I argue that, there is need of two communities to co-exist together, whether they like it or not. The Akobo County will not be enjoyed by one community without the other community. This conflict will be resolved by the elites, intelligentsia and the traditional leaders of both communities with the help of State government. Yes, the Ciro-Anyuak clan lost hundreds if not thousands of precious lives at the hands of Lou-Nuer-Mor elites and intelligentsia groups. This should now be considered as history, but it should never be repeated again. We should not blame both communities for events of the past. I argue that this is an era to move on, and leave the past behind. Both communities have been part of many atrocities and aberrations. However, let us not allow the past to influence our present co-existence. Let both communities open a new page and move on. Moreover, I also propose a peace reconciliation conference between the two communities in the near future. Therefore; I am proposing a strategy for resolution to the conflict in Akobo as following-:

1. Recognition and acceptance from the Lou-Nuer-Mor that, Akobo-Ciro-Anyuaks were and still are the indigenous inhabitants of the land of Akobo.

2. To resolve the dispute of Akobo-Ciro-Anyuak who were not allowed to build in their previous places by Lou-Nuer-Mor in Akobo.

3. Tribal chiefs, civil society groups and county authorities to form an organization to deal with the issue of cattle grazing rights.

4. Drawing an articulated historical political and social charter of understanding between the Akobo-Ciro-Anyuak and Luo-Nuer-Mor communities.

5. The Lou-Nuer-Mor must evacuate all the areas of Akobo-Ciro-Anyuak previous areas immediately without delay to pave the way for the Akobo-Ciro-Anyuak returnees, IDPs and refugees to return their homes.

6. Political power sharing arrangements must be established between Akobo-Ciro-Anyuak and Luo-Nuer-Mor to reflect the ethnic diversity and rainbow of Akobo County.

7. Respect of the richness of each ethnic community's cultural diversity.

8. The Akobo-Ciro-Anyuaks are willing to adhere to power sharing arrangements and will co-exist in harmony and peacefully with the Lou-Nuer-Mor without any prejudice and segregation in Akobo County.

9. To preserve the Akobo-Ciro-Anyuak political right in key political decision making in Akobo County affairs without any prejudice.

10. Sustainable encouragement of dialogue and negotiation between the Akobo-Ciro-Anyuak and Lou-Nuer-Mor as the only mechanism for co-existence between the two ethnic communities.

Akobo Anyuak Conference

Since the British colonial era, the Akobo District historically and traditionally continues to be known as the Anyuak District since its establishment in 1910. At the end of the 1940s and early 1950s, the British District Commissioners of Fangak and Akobo decided to annex the

117

greater Lou-Nuer area to the Akobo district claiming difficulty in administration from the Fangak District. That is how the greater Lou-Nuer came to be part and parcel of the Akobo District.

The first Lou-Nuer-Mor settlers to come to Akobo district were: Mr. Kok Diang, grandfather of prominent politician, Dr. Riek Gai Kok, Deng Jok, Lual Thian the grandfather of Brigadier General Kat Gang Lual Thian who settled at Kaibuy. Last of the initial group was Nyieng Chamjok, grandfather of Eng. Chamjok Chung living at Meer. These are the families recognized by the Ciro/Anyuak people known as Akobo Anyuak.

It is worthy of note here that the Lou-Nuer community has two major clans, namely the Lou-Nuer-Mor and Lou-Nuer-Gon. The Gon clan is divided into two sub-clans namely, Chan-Jaak in Uruo County and Gat Bail in Nyirol County. The Anyuak of Akobo has three major clans: Ciro, Nyikany and Ojwa.

Under the theme: **"Where there is no vision people perish,"** the Akobo Anyuak consultative conference was conducted between December 27–29, 2012 at Bor, Jonglei State. During a three days deliberation, the conference decided several important recommendations stating that the Akobo-Anyuak people aspire to live in peace with their neighbors and will collaborate with all the communities of Jonglei State at large to achieve lasting peace. Also according to South Sudan constitution, the land belongs to the community. Based on this principle, the Akobo Anyuak resolved to respect the constitution and that the Anyuak Community in Akobo and the three families: Lou-Nuer-Mor (Kok Diang) at Deng Jok; Lual Thian at Kaibuy; and Nyang Chamjok at Meer have authority over use of land. Addition the Akobo town belongs to any South Sudanese citizen for residential and business purposes.

Anyuak Kingdom Political Pioneers

The Anyuak kingdom has benefitted from the missionary work in 1930s by the American Mission which later on came to be known as the Presbyterian Church of the United States (PC/USA). These efforts provided Anyuak children education and access to a world aspect. They not only gained education, but they were also Christianized and took Biblical names.

The first political pioneers were:

1.   Ambassador Philip Obang Oywie (Adongo Clan-Pochalla) (British educated)

2.   Mr. Simon Morris Didumo (Cham Clan- Pochalla, born in Ethiopia) (American educated)

3.   Mr. Paul Andei Othow (Ciro Clan- Akobo) (American educated)

4.   Crd. Paul Niywory Ojulo (Adongo Clan-Pochalla) (ANYANYA ONE Leader of Upper Nile Province

5.   Crd. Joseph Otio Akwan (Adongo Clan- Pochalla) (The Anyanya Leader in Upper Nile Province and second Commander of General Joseph Lago)

6.   Gen. David Okwier Akwei (Adongo Clan- Pochalla)

7.   Eng. David Ojulo Agwo (Ciro Clan-Akobo)

8.   Brigadier General (Rt.) Stephen Ogut Obongo (Ciro Clan-Akobo). This is just to mention a few of the pioneers.

In 2010 the first ever Anyuak woman joined political arena when His Excellency Governor Kuol Manyang Juk appointed a Minister for Cooperatives and Rural Development in Jonglei. She is Mrs. Apoudho Ojulo (Ciro-Anyuak clan), the first South Sudanese Anyuak female to complete her education in 1982 at the Malakal Institute of Education as a primary education teacher.

In 2012, Mrs. Rachael Anok Omot (Ciro Clan, Akobo) was appointed by His Excellency Governor Kuol Manyang Juk to become the second Anyuak woman to enter politics as a Minster for Gender and Social Development up to now.

The white man did not only bring the church to the Anyuak Kingdom but also brought politics and government.

The Arab Muslims had influenced the country for trade and their religion. The white man benefitted the Anyuak Kingdom in the important areas of education and translation of the Bible into the Anyuak mother tongue. Most significantly Dr. Conradin Perner, known by the Anyuak name, Kwacakworo, has written volumes about the anthropological and sociological background of the Anyuak Kingdom. He deserves great credit for the wonderful historic work he has done for our Anyuak Kingdom. I strongly recommend to the Anyuak Kingdom leadership at home and in the Diaspora to honor the missionaries and Dr. Conradin Perner in the near future.

Chapter 8

Final Words

I write this last chapter, especially to those of you who are refugees, to encourage you. Yes, I was a refugee in Australia for nine years, but in 2005, I was appointed a Member of Parliament (MP) by the GOSS representing my constituency Akobo, County in Bor, Jonglei State Transitional Assembly. The peace that year stipulated 20% South Sudanese representation in all the national ministries including the Ministry of Foreign Affairs (MAF). Dr. Lam Akol became the first ever South Sudanese Minister of Foreign Affairs in the history of modern Sudan. He was a most experienced and competent gentleman, educated in Britain, and the first among seven other South Sudanese Ministers.

Dr. Lam Akol was the only one to implement the 20% quota in the MFA. In 2006, I was among the first of those who applied and submitted a resume for an MFA post. After screening and assessment of credentials, I was appointed at the rank of Minister plenipotentiary. My first assignment was in the Directorate of Protocol headed by His Excellency Ambassador Ali Yousif, a liberal Northern Sudanese. In 2007- 2009 I was the Deputy Director of Ceremonies.

On 9th July 2009, I was posted to Ankara, Turkey as the first ever South Sudanese from the MFA to be posted to this country as Deputy Chief of Mission. I struggled and debated with myself whether I should take it or not, however, after consulting with my wife and some close friends, I was advised to take the position and I did for three reasons:-

1. I did not have somebody to back me up in either the national Government or in the GOSS, where it is whom you know, and not what you know.

2. Financial hardship: I was receiving seven hundred Sudanese Pounds per month, equivalent to $300.00.

3. Experience: the most important factor.

Prior my departure to Ankara, I heard that Ambassador Omar Hider Abuziad was nominated as designated Ambassador of Sudan to Ankara, Turkey. While he was waiting for his acceptance (*agremia*) by the Turkish Government, we met over a cup of coffee. I told him that, I would be travelling on 7th July. He responded that he would be very happy working with me, and he hoped our working relationship would be cordial and friendly. When he arrived in Ankara a month later, I was serving as Chargé d'Affaires Interim. We commenced our work and in six months he called me for a meeting with other diplomats and expressed his gratitude. He said he was not expecting to have such a pleasant and cordial working relations with a South Sudanese. He had assumed our working relations would be difficult.

Our friendship grew over cups of tea in his house and mine so that our families also bonded. Once South Sudanese diplomats called the house and asked my wife: "Where's Dhano." She responded: "He's out with the Chief of Mission." They were surprised because Ambassador Abuzaid is a northern Sudanese.

Ambassador Abuzaid had a good system of having a cup of tea with the diplomatic staff when we arrived each morning for discussion of events and planning. After a half hour, everybody went to work well informed. This cordial relationship went very well until March, 2011, when the results of a referendum were announced and the news came of the succession of South Sudan. This required South Sudanese diplomats to report to MFA headquarters in Khartoum, Sudan.

On 30th December, 2010, I had been sitting with the ambassador when his secretary said the Turkish Ministry of Foreign Affairs was asking to speak to the Deputy of Chief Mission from South Sudan. The ambassador said to go ahead with the call and the Turkish MFA said they had a diplomat nominated to be Consul in Juba who would monitor the referendum voting and that they had received an approval from the MFA in Khartoum. I said: "Okay. Give me some time and I will be back to you." I went to inform Ambassador Omar Hider Abuzaid. He gave the okay.

In my work experience in the embassy, on occasion Northern Sudanese diplomats would want to discuss sensitive issues. Due to historical mistrust, they opted to go outside away from me and I definitely felt that. In October 2010, Honorable Mr. Ali Ahamd Karti, Minister of Foreign Affairs in the Islamist regime, was invited by his Turkish counterpart, Dr. Ahmet Davutoglu, Minister of Foreign Affairs, for a two-day state visit. I was included in the delegation, something I was not expecting. From our Ministry of Foreign Affairs there was Ambassador Majak Philemon Majok, the Director of European Affairs, and a South Sudanese. The second day, we had meeting with President Abdullah Gul, the President of the Republic of Turkey. The meeting centered on the political developments in Sudan in general, and on South Sudan in particular, focusing mainly on the referendum. I could see that President Gull was well briefed by his MFA. He asked Honorable Karti, "Please, tell me. What is the percentage of the South Sudanese who may vote for secession?" Mr. Karti responded: "Only a handful of people." *I wanted to laugh, but*

I controlled myself. I knew he was mistaken. I knew if the referendum was fair and transparent, more than 80% of the South Sudanese would vote in favor of Independence; the actual outcome was 98%.

The Present Crisis

As I complete the writing of this book, my beloved country of South Sudan is in a devastating humanitarian crisis. On 15th December 2013, the former Vice President Dr. Riek Machar was accused by the government of South Sudan of carrying out an attempted coup d'état to overthrow the democratically-elected civilian President Silva Kiir Mayardit who currently serves as the first President of the Republic of South Sudan since our independence in 2011. This attempted coup led to outbreaks of violence around the country. During the violent conflict, the United Nations agencies estimated that 800,000 South Sudanese became Internal Displaced Peoples (IDPS), and more than 1,000 South Sudanese were killed. I strongly believe that the solution will be for the two rivaling parties to sit together and dialogue to resolve this political conflict amicably. The South Sudanese people have suffered for long time, and they do not deserve to suffer again after attaining their precious independence from the Arab-Islamic regime of Sudan.

Sadly as a result of the current conflict, hundreds of thousands of South Sudanese have become refugees in

Uganda, Kenya, Sudan, Ethiopia, and in other neighboring countries. In the near future, those South Sudanese who have been affected by the conflict may get an opportunity to be resettled by the United Nations High Commission for Refugees (UNHCR) for the sake of security and protection. Thus a new generation of refugees will be resettled in third countries namely Australia, Canada, Europe, and the United States of America. Again it is my hope in writing this book is that it will be of significance to South Sudanese in the Diasporia and torefugee service providers working with the continuing influx of refugees and immigrants around the globe.

Dhanojak Obongo

Notes on Sources

1. Alier A. (2003) *Southern Sudan: Too Many Agreements Dishonored*, 2nd Ed. Khartoum, Sudan.

2. Nikkle, Mark(1992) *Dinka and Christianity.*

3. Perner, Conradin (1990) *Anyuak Living on Earth in the Sky: The Anyuak an Analytic Account of History and Culture of a Nilotic People, Volumes 1 & 2.*

4. Evans- Pritchard, E.E(1942) *The Nuer Religion.*

5. Deng, F.M. (1990) *War of Visions:Conflict of Identities in the Sudan.*

6. Evans-Pritchard, E.E (1942) *The Political System of the Anyuak of Anglo-Egyptian Sudan.*

7. Wai, Dunstan. (1981) *The African – Arab Conflict in the Sudan*

8. Poggo, Scopas S. (2009)*The First Sudanese civil war- Africans, Arabs, and Israelis in the Southern Sudan 1955- 1972.*

9. Willis, C.A. (1995) *The Upper Nile Province Handbook- A Report on Peoples and Government in the Southern Sudan, 1931.*

10. Malwal, Bona. (1985) *The Sudan A Second Challenge to Nationhood.*

11. Malwal, B. (1981) *People and Power in Sudan.* London: Ithaca Press

12. *Akol, Lam (2007)Southern Sudan- Colonialism, Resistance and Autonom,* The Red Sea Press, Inc.

13. *"South Sudanese Women's Priorities(2011)/ Invest" in Women Develop South Sudan*

14. Collins, Robert O.(*1956) "History of the Anyuak" 1956./ www.akobociro.net*

15. *New African Magazine (May, 1995).*
16. *Sudantribune.com/*article 49871 /February 6, 2014
17. *Informants Sources:-*
    - *Obongo, Stephen Oguot. Informant and interviewed by Dhano ObongoNov. 2009.*

    - *Rev. Abulla oElijah Omot. Informant.*

    - *Mrs.Ochang, Rebecca Amot. Informant.*

    - *Www- akobo-ciro.org websites.*

    - *Sudan Country profile / website*

    - *www.nationsonline.org/ oneworld/ Sudan.htm*

    - *South Sudan Government Offical website*

    - *Laws of the Republic of South Sudan/ The Transitional Constitution , 2011*

    - *www.alrakoba.net/ Radio Sawaa/ 20/07/2013*